W9-CCJ-429

ACTIONS
SPEAK
LOUDER
THAN
VERBS

ACTIONS SPEAK LOUDER THAN VERBS

Herb Miller

ABINGDON PRESS
NASHVILLE

ACTIONS SPEAK LOUDER THAN VERBS

Copyright © 1989 by Abingdon Press

This book is printed on acid-free paper.

Library of Congress Cataloging-in-Publication Data

MILLER, HERB.
Actions speak louder than verbs / Herb Miller.
p. cm.
Bibliography: p.
ISBN 0-687-00712-7 (pbk. : alk. paper)
1. Jesus Christ—Words—Meditations. 2. Jesus Christ—Teachings—Meditations. I. Title.
BT306.M53   1989   88-22642
248.4'8663—dc19   CIP

Scripture quotations marked RSV are from the Revised Standard Version of the Bible, copyright 1946, 1952, 1971 by the Division of Christian Education of the National Council of Churches of Christ in the USA. Used by permission.

Scripture quotations noted ANT are from the Amplified New Testament, © The Lockman Foundation 1954, 1958, 1987.

Those marked KJV are from the King James Version of the Bible.

Manufactured by the Parthenon Press at
Nashville, Tennessee, United States of America

*To Floyd and Janet Legler
of Remington, Indiana—the most action oriented disciples I know*

ACKNOWLEDGMENTS

Of the countless persons who helped make this book possible, two deserve special mention: Barbara Miller, who assisted with the biblical research, and Debi Blake, whose nimble fingers translated scribbles to print.

CONTENTS

INTRODUCTION

How is your French?" an African tourist asked his guide as they entered an area in which that language predominated.

"Excellent," replied the interpreter. "All except the verbs." That's quite an exception; a language without verbs loses all its action. The research on which this book is based grew out of a similar observation: The verbs people use photograph the action based side of their lives and thus reveal people's most fundamental beliefs. That observation led to the question, "What verbs did Jesus use?"

The ten verbs in these ten chapters are not the *only* verbs Jesus used, but they are the dominant ones. An exhaustive study of every verb the New Testament reports Jesus' having used indicates that the others cluster logically under these ten. Several chapters, therefore, list related verbs and illustrate how those related verbs fit in with the chapter's primary verb. The original manuscript records of Jesus' words were, of course, written in Greek. All the verbs in these chapters are taken from the Revised Standard Version of that New Testament Greek. While these English verbs are not the only way to translate the original Greek verbs, they are widely accepted by contemporary scholars.

Each chapter provides sample texts in which Jesus used that chapter's primary verb. In a few instances, one or more of the texts quoted in the "Samples from Jesus' Teachings" section does not literally contain that verb. In each of the texts cited in those sections, however, virtually all biblical scholars and standard Bible commentaries say that this verb is what Jesus is teaching in these verses. A good example is found in chapter 1 where "unless you turn" in Matthew 18:3-4 is believed by scholars to mean the same as "repent" found in Matthew 4:17 and elsewhere. Since all biblical interpretation is ultimately personal, the reader is free to disagree or to agree with these text samples as illustrations of the chapter's primary verb.

Several chapters contain a section entitled "Related Verbs Jesus Used." Whether the texts quoted in the sections actually are related to the chapter's primary verb is open to personal opinion and debate. The research on which this book is based surfaced *every* verb Jesus used. Therefore, rather than leaving out several verbs that are either obvious synonyms or, in my opinion, appear to be closely related to the chapter's primary verb, it seemed best to quote all of them. This inclusion in the book of *all the verbs Jesus used* allows the reader to agree, to disagree, or to raise questions with far greater ease than would have been possible if some of them had been excluded.

Christianity contains many important nouns—pew, pulpit, Sunday school, denomination. The adjectives convey meaning, too—holy, dedicated, sincere. But the verbs power the action— follow, serve, love, forgive. Jesus did not primarily ask people to *think* things. He called them to *do* things. This does not mean that the nouns of our faith do not matter, but if we know the nouns and never learn the verbs, we have something other than *Christian* faith. By getting in touch with his great verbs, we move closer to the Person behind the verbs. This inevitably moves us toward new life by moving us toward new ways of thinking and acting.

PART I

How to Connect with God's Creative Energy

Chapter 1

REPENT: WINNING IS NOT ENOUGH!

Two Kentucky farmers who owned racing stables had developed a keen rivalry. One spring, each of them entered a horse in a local steeplechase. Thinking that a professional rider might help him outdo his friend, one of the farmers engaged a crack jockey. The two horses were leading the race at the last fence, but it proved too tough for them. Both horses fell, unseating their riders. But this calamity did not stop the professional jockey. He quickly remounted and won the race.

Returning triumphant to the paddock, the jockey found the farmer who had hired him fuming with rage. "What's the matter?" the jockey asked. "I won, didn't I?"

"Oh, yes," roared the farmer. "You won all right, but you still don't know, do you?"

"Know what?" asked the jockey.

"You won the race on the wrong horse."

While this situation does not occur often at horse races, it happens in every human life. Each of us, trying hard to win the race, tends to climb on the wrong horse. If we do not discover our error, we cross the finish line a triumphant failure. Jesus labels this faulty human reflex with a noun from the Old Testament: *sin*. He says an Old Testament verb is the only cure for it: *repent*.

Samples from Jesus' Teachings

Repent, for the kingdom of heaven is at hand. (Matthew 4:17)

The time is fulfilled, and the kingdom of God is at hand; repent, and believe in the gospel. (Mark 1:15)

Truly, I say to you, unless you turn and become like children, you will never enter the kingdom of heaven. Whoever humbles himself like this child, he is the greatest in the kingdom of heaven. (Matthew 18:3-4)

Or those eighteen upon whom the tower in Siloam fell and killed them, do you think that they were worse offenders than all the others who dwelt in Jerusalem? I tell you, No; but unless you repent you will all likewise perish. (Luke 13:4-5; for full picture, read Luke 13:1-9)

And if your hand or your foot causes you to sin, cut it off and throw it away; it is better for you to enter life maimed or lame than with two hands or two feet to be thrown into the eternal fire. And if your eye causes you to sin, pluck it out and throw it away; it is better for you to enter life with one eye than with two eyes to be thrown into the hell of fire. (Matthew 18:8-9; see also Mark 9:43-48)

Woe to you, scribes and Pharisees, hypocrites! for you tithe mint and dill and cummin, and have neglected the weightier matters of the law, justice and mercy and faith; these you ought to have done, without neglecting the others. You blind guides, straining out a gnat and swallowing a camel!
Woe to you, scribes and Pharisees, hypocrites! for you are like whitewashed tombs, which outwardly appear beautiful, but within they are full of dead men's bones and all uncleanness. So you also outwardly appear righteous to men, but within you are full of hypocrisy and iniquity.
. . . You serpents, you brood of vipers, how are you to escape being sentenced to hell? (Matthew 23:23-24, 27-28, 33; for full picture, read Matthew 23:23-33)

Related Verbs Jesus Used

Render to God. "Render to Caesar the things that are Caesar's, and to God the things that are God's" (Mark 12:17). This statement is also found in Luke 20:25.

Love God. "The first [commandment] is, 'Hear, O Israel: The Lord our God, the Lord is one; and you shall love the Lord your God with all your heart, and with all your soul, and with all your mind, and with all your strength.' The second is this, 'You shall love your neighbor as yourself.' There is no other commandment greater than these" (Mark 12:29-30). See also Luke 10:25-28.

Worship God. "It is written, 'You shall worship the Lord your God, and him only shall you serve' " Luke 4:8). See also John 2:14-16.

Hear me and *believe* God. "Truly, truly, I say to you, he who hears my word and believes him who sent me, has eternal life; he does not come into judgment, but has passed from death to life" (John 5:24). See also John 5:39-44.

Do not tempt God. "It is said, 'You shall not tempt the Lord your God'" Luke 4:12).

Do not be a slave to sin. "Truly, truly, I say to you, every one who commits sin is a slave to sin" (John 8:34).

Seek new birth. "Truly, truly, I say to you, unless one is born anew, he cannot see the kingdom of God" (John 3:3). For the full picture, read John 3:1-8.

Singular and Plural Repentance

We can get on the wrong horse in two different ways: as individuals and as a group. The most obvious need for repentance is singular.

A wealthy woman who lived in a lavish home frequently grumbled to her maid, "I just need to get away from it all for a while."

One day the maid finally found the courage to ask, "What is it that you need to get away from?" Getting a vague answer, she added, "Maybe what you need to get away from is yourself."

A cartoon delivered the same punch by picturing a man whose physician examined him and said, "You have a very serious problem. You are allergic to yourself." Often, our worst enemy is within rather than outside us. Few people will ever need an organ transplant, but many of us need a personality transplant.

A seminary professor gave this prescription to her students: "Be yourself—unless you are a jerk, in which case you should be someone else!" That advice is consistent with the verb Jesus used in the preaching with which he launched his ministry: *repent!* (see Matt. 4:17 and Mark 1:15). The remainder of the New Testament is a recurrent story of people who decided that they were on the wrong horse. By their turning in a new direction, God's creative energy began flowing through them, and they became something much more than they could have been through their own intelligence and effort.

The other way we can get on the wrong horse is corporately—as a group, as a culture, as a nation, or as an entire civilization. The twentieth century has witnessed enormous human progress in advances in knowledge, lengthened life spans, increased housing quality, and higher standards of living. We have explored the earth and oceans. We have visited the moon and probed the planets. But do people treat one another better? Is war less of a threat? Has inequality been dethroned? Human greed seems as powerful as ever. Governments still as easily become slaves to their baser selves. Hitler's Germany in which millions of Jews were killed is one example. South African apartheid is another. Each of us could cite a dozen more examples. A biologist may have been right when he announced, "I have discovered the missing link between the anthropoid apes and civilized humans. It is us!"

Dwight D. Eisenhower said in his January 20, 1953, inaugural address, "Whatever America hopes to bring to pass in the world must first come to pass in the heart of America" (*The International Thesaurus of Quotations*). Some repentance must be plural, corporate, group, or governmental. Without that, a one at a time change of heart can fall short of real change. It can change hearts without changing the group systems in which those hearts beat.

Repent of What?

Jesus says that the failure to repent brings dire consequences: "Unless you repent you will all likewise perish" (Luke 13:5). But of what, exactly, should we repent? In his harsh story about one son who repented and another who didn't, Jesus uses the Greek word *metanoia* for repentance (see Matt. 21:28-32). It means a change of mind, deciding to turn around and go in a different direction. What wrong direction must we reverse?

The apostle Paul, one of our most respected interpreters of the mind of Christ, says that becoming a Christian involves becoming a totally new person, "the old has passed away, behold, the new has come" (II Cor. 5:17). Becoming a Christian is not like tacking aluminum siding onto your house; it is like burning the house down and building a steel and glass skyscraper over the foundation. But what, exactly, was wrong with the house?

The answer is packed into one of the most misunderstood words in the Bible—*sin*. Much of our failure to grasp the full meaning of *repent* arises from confusing the basic singular word—*sin*—with the plural secondary word—*sins*. *Sin* and *sins* mean two entirely different things. Failure to make that distinction leads us to paint a thin coat of morals and ethics over our personal prejudices and call it Christianity.

Sin Singular. When Mark Twain and his daughter traveled across Europe together, they were honored at every stop. Royalty and famous artists and scientists hosted them. Near the end of the trip, Twain's daughter said, "Papa, you know everybody but God, don't you?" That quip is a good definition of sin singular. Each of us has a basic predisposition to focusing our lives in directions other than toward God.

Sin singular inclines us to violate the first Commandment and substitute something else for a relationship with God. Andy Warhol once said, "I am a deeply superficial person." He is not alone. We all struggle to overcome our basic superficiality. The theological description of that enemy within is "original sin."

The average child begins to talk between fourteen and eighteen months after birth. Regardless of sex, the first word spoken is usually "dada." In first-century Palestine, a Jewish child of that age usually said, "Ab-ab" for Abba, the Aramaic equivalent of Daddy. Jesus told his disciples to address God that way, as a loving parent. He said that everyone who does not know God in that way needs to repent and move in that direction.

Sigmund Freud, the father of modern psychiatry, once said, "I have found little that is good about human beings. In my experience, most of them are trash." Jesus says that we are trash, that we have a basic sinful bent. But unlike Freud, Jesus says we are redeemable trash. We can be recycled and born again into a better product than we were the first time. But in order to arrive at that *renewed* condition, we have to repent of not relating to God.

Sins Plural. Sin, as in "original sin," is always singular. When Jesus urges people to repent of sin, he is asking them to repent of not relating to God. The more commonly used English term derived from the primary word *sins* is infinitely plural. In living out our basic reflex—sin—we have an unlimited number of optional actions by which we may make something other than God the guiding relationship of our life. These actions (sins) come in two different modalities: thinking and doing. Lust, for example, is a thinking sin; whereas adultery is a doing sin. Hatred is a thinking sin; murder is a doing sin. Greed is a thinking sin; stealing is a doing sin.

In contrast to the other teachers of his day, Jesus said that we need to repent of thinking sins as well as of doing sins. Why? Because thinking sins also signify that we are putting something else in place of God. For Jesus, the central issue is always the attitudinal condition of the heart, not just the actions that emanate from the heart. This does not mean that lust has the same consequence as adultery. Obviously, it does not, but it is equally a sin. Getting on the wrong horse begins by either accidentally or intentionally thinking about getting on the wrong horse.

Summary of the difference between sin singular and sins plural. Gallup Poll studies report that 40 percent of the citizens of the United States currently attend worship each week. This number is down from 49 percent in 1959. The Roman Catholic Church tags the behavior of the other 60 percent a sin (as in sins plural). But the primary sin here is breaking relationship with God (sin singular). Jesus says that we need to repent of both.

Suddenly or Slowly?

The verb *repent* keeps close company with another heavyweight biblical and theological term, *conversion*. Conversion is turning away from one's former habits and beginning to rely on God's help. This may be sudden, or it may be a gradually developing relationship with God.

Some people repent instantly, as Paul did on the Damascus Road (Acts 9:3-6). For others, repentance is gradual, like that of the apostles on the road to Emmaus who finally realized that Christ was among them at the end of a long journey (Luke 24:13-43). When the "instantly converted" and the "gradually converted" come together, they find it difficult to communicate their experiences. Those who have a sudden overwhelming conversion are tempted to believe that theirs is the only true doorway to God. Yet, both types of repentance can result in new life.

Free Gas for the Trip

During his early manhood, John Newton of England developed several crippling habits—sexual excess, drunkenness, and drug addiction. Unable to disentangle himself from these parasitic habits, he felt his life being eaten away. Then, through some kind words from a friend and the intervention of a minister, John Newton's habits began to change. He became a totally different person. He wrote a description of this alteration in the words of a hymn.

> Amazing grace! how sweet the sound,
> That saved a wretch like me!
> I once was lost, but now am found,
> Was blind, but now I see.

Newton used another seventy-five cent theological word, without which we cannot fully comprehend the verb *repent—grace*. There is one sense in which repentance is an inside job. We must decide; nobody can decide for us. Yet, there is another sense in which the fuel tank that powers repentance is always filled from the outside, free of charge. We do not repent by our own power alone. It is a joint project. The Bible calls that experience grace. Innately, because of "original sin," we tend to want the wrong things. We tend to get on the wrong horse and try to win races that do not ultimately matter. Grace, that mysterious unexplainable power that comes from somewhere outside ourselves, lets us begin to see the difference between the horses. By the power of grace, we start wanting the right things.

A minister who found himself in a strange part of his city needed some cash. Obtaining directions to a branch bank he had never been to before, he rushed in, filled out the proper forms, and handed them to the teller. She surprised him by refusing them. "What's the problem?" he asked. "I'm sure I have money in the account."

"I am sure you do, sir," she replied. "But you are at the wrong bank. Your bank is across the street."[1] Whether we do it slowly or quickly, by Damascus or Emmaus, repentance begins with the moment we decide that we are at the wrong bank and decide to cross the street. That does not happen by our own intelligence and power alone; God helps us by providing insight to light the way. The Bible calls this grace.

To Be Specific

The Ten Commandments adequately list the basic sins plural— stealing, murder, lying and so on. The rest of the Bible, and countless other books, illustrate these sins. But less obvious sins can be equally dangerous as these.

Do we need to repent of substituting a connection with the Church for a connection with God? A national church leader, drinking coffee at a restaurant counter, was scribbling ideas on a yellow pad. A patron in the next chair had been talking with the waitress. When she left to wait on other customers, he tried to strike up a conversation with the denominational executive. "What kind of work are you in?" he asked. "Are you an accountant?"

After a lengthy explanation, the man still looked puzzled. Several seconds of silence passed. The minister had started writing again when the man hit him with an unexpected question, "Are you a Christian?"

Taken aback and realizing that his new friend intended to take the conversation down a road he did not want to travel, the pastor fired a question in return. "Wouldn't it be a little strange for me to be running a national church organization if I were not a Christian?"

"Not necessarily," the man said.

His irritating insight is accurate. We can fail to stay connected with God, even in full-time service to his church. That is precisely the problem Martin Luther had to fix in the Protestant Reformation of the early 1500s. People's commitment to the Church exceeded their commitment to God.

In the year 324, Christianity became popular after Emperor Constantine made it the official state religion. He reportedly began this process by baptizing twelve thousand men, women, and children. To encourage their conversion, he offered each twenty gold pieces and a white baptismal robe.[2] Repentance that actually brings new life must be more personal than this, and it must be deeper than merely joining or attending church.

Do we need to repent of phony repentance? A story involving the familiar Roman Catholic penance of "making the stations of the cross" involves two Manhattan ladies of the evening who decided to change their ways. Entering the Franciscan church on West 31st Street, one made her confession. She emerged with a puzzled look and waited while her friend entered the confessional. She, too, came out with a questioning look on her face. After they were outside the building, the first said to the second, "What did he say to you?"

"He told me to make the stations."

"That's funny," said the second. "He told me the same thing. What did he mean?"

"I don't get it," said the first. "But he must know what he's doing, so let's get going. You hit Penn Station and I'll hit Grand Central. It certainly is an odd way to reform."

Protestants have circulated many jokes of that sort, the punch line often describing a Catholic who comes to confession drunk and asks forgiveness, then goes out and does the same thing next week, expecting to be forgiven again. But a close scrutiny of reality shows little Protestant superiority in this behavior. Every church has people who repeatedly admit that they have not acted as they should, but they go right on repeating the same behavior. What many need to repent of more than anything else is a "dieter's repentance"—one that doesn't last.

Albert Camus put his finger on one of the reasons for this behavior in his book *The Fall*. The leading character, Clemence, feels he must find a way to divert the public eye from himself. He discovers that if he confesses his sins, people stop judging him and start concentrating on their own sins. A good many people have discovered this effective ploy. Their confessions become an effective way to manipulate other people into not criticizing them. Used in that way, honesty becomes a deceitful tool to evade scrutiny from the outside and to avoid reform on the inside.

Churches devote much time to teaching the good news that God always forgives. That is appropriate, and we easily forget it. But the other side of that truth too often goes neglected. Hearts can grow hardened from phony repentance. When we say we are wrong but are still not relating to God in ways that allow us to change, we can lose the ability to repent.

When John the Baptist said, "Bear fruits that befit repentance" (Luke 3:8) he was charging deeply religious leaders with phony repentance. Jesus picked up the same theme with the same crowd: "Repent, for the kingdom of heaven is at hand" (Matt. 3:2) You cannot attend a grand ball in a jogging suit and tennis shoes. What happens after repentance is like a check clearing the bank—it proves whether the repentance was real.

Do we need to repent of the contemporary hesitancy to identify our negative tendencies? Popular sentiment says that the church should be positive, not negative. It should concentrate on good news, not bad news. Forget about sin; celebrate salvation. Negativism probably deserves all the negative press it gets. Yet, some matters cannot be fully addressed except through negative illustration. How can you suggest that people repent without telling them they are on the wrong horse?

Each of the countless villages of Switzerland has a church that stands tall above the houses. Most of these churches have a clock on at least one side of the steeple; some have a clock on two or all four sides. Down through the centuries, someone in the town had to know the right time. Otherwise, the entire village would become hopelessly confused about when to do what.

History tells us that in every era—Nazi Germany in the 1930s, for example—when the Church does not stand tall and speak clearly regarding what time it is, everyone in town eventually gets into big trouble. Calling us to repentance, both as a society and as individuals, is one of the most important functions that churches carry out on behalf of Christ. If our churches do not do this, who will? Certainly not governments—they only tax and regulate us. Certainly not business—it only provides us with jobs, goods, and services. Certainly not schools—they only educate us.

In carrying out this function, the Church cannot avoid some negatives. Review the Ten Commandments. Even God found it difficult to warn people against getting on the wrong horse without using some negative language. Maimonides, a thirteenth-century Jewish philosopher, said that a doctor's job is to cure sometimes and to comfort always. To be effective in the healing task, the Church often needs to *dis*comfort in order to cure. Sometimes, being negative is positive.

Do we need to repent of a false sense of superiority? During the summer of 1986, two ships collided in the Black Sea, and many lives were lost. An investigation revealed an even deeper aspect of the tragedy. Both captains knew that the other ship was close by. Either could have taken evasive action, but the reports told that neither would give way to the other. Both were too proud to make the first move. By the time they saw that a crash was inevitable, it was too late. Hundreds of passengers ended up in the icy waters.

A pride-filled attitude of superiority is one of original sin's most destructive by-products because it distorts reality. We can detect this trait in ourselves by asking whether we ever think in any of the following ways. When you take a long time to do something, you're slow. When I take a long time, I'm thorough. When you don't do it, you're lazy. When I don't do it, I'm busy. When you do it without being asked, you're overstepping your authority. When I go ahead and do it, that's initiative. When you state your opinion strongly, you're bull-headed. When I do that, I'm firm. When you overlook rules of etiquette, you're rude. When I do, I'm just eccentric. When your family has money, you're greedy. When mine does, we are successful.

After hearing a scorching sermon about personal responsibility, a woman said, "I don't think there is much wrong with us."

The young, inexperienced pastor responded like John the Baptist,

"That is the biggest thing that is wrong with our church. We don't think there is anything wrong with us."

That is precisely what happened to the Pharisees. Convinced that they had reached the heights of spiritual perfection, they were willing to cry out to Pontius Pilate, "His blood be on us and on our children" (Matt. 27:25) and "Let him be crucified" (Matt. 27:23). It was for people who carried this distorted view of reality, stemming from false pride, that Jesus said out of his agony on the cross, "Father, forgive them; for they know not what they do" (Luke 23:34).

It was not the prodigal sons of the world who nailed Christ to a wooden cross; it was the elder brothers who felt that they had arrived at spiritual superiority. The apostle Paul had a proper perspective of reality when he said, "I press on toward the goal for the prize of the upward call of God in Christ Jesus" (Phil. 3:14). That is a great motto. However, anytime you think you have obtained the goal, that is a sure sign you haven't. To repent means that we turn in the direction of a perfect connection with God. It never means that we have arrived there.

Do we need to repent of negative thinking about our past? Voltaire said, "The repentance of man is accepted by God as a virtue."[3] This philosophical observation summarizes the meaning in two other theological terms without which we cannot fully understand the verb *repent—atonement* and *forgiveness of sins* (Luke 24:47). When we connect with God in repentance, God counts our bad past as a good past. Therefore, it is sinful (ungodly) for us to keep thinking negatively about our past.

Charles L. Allen tells the delightful story of a boy who laboriously crafted a beautiful sailboat but lost it in a gust of wind on a big lake. Weeks later, the boy was passing a toy store and saw his boat for sale in the window. After a quick trip home to rob his bank, he eagerly bought the little boat. Walking home with his arms wrapped around it, he said, "Little boat, you are mine. I made you, and I bought you." Allen concludes the story by stating, "That is what God says to each of us. He made us, and with the life of His Son He bought us. We are God's persons."[4]

We often say that people should get exactly what they deserve. We don't really mean that. All of us want what's coming to us on the positive side of the ledger; for example, we want to receive the full salary we earn. However, none of us wants to receive what we earn through our past negative behavior. Thanks to the grace of atonement, we get much more than we deserve. If we repent, we get remission of sins. In computer terminology, we get a deleted past and a clean disk.

Do we need to repent of negative thinking about our future? For most people, quality of life is determined less by what they think about their past than by how they think about their future. In the biblical story of Noah, forty days of rain put the highest peaks under water. When it was time to leave the ark, Noah sent out a dove. The first time out, the dove flew around a while and came back. The second time out, it returned with an olive branch in its beak. On the third flight, the bird did not return. Finding dry land, it began a new life. Shortly afterward, Noah did the same.

That story is much more than a Jewish version of ancient history. It pictures God's dealings with each of us. No matter how many mistakes we make or how dreary the rain, God hangs a rainbow in our future. He always gives us a chance to start over, to begin a new life.

If we repent of concentrating on the rain instead of the rainbow, we find that the old Chinese proverb is right: "Failure can be the first step toward success." To be restored in our connection with God means to be "re-storied" by seeing a new future, which includes greater experiences than we could have earned for ourselves. Being restored also involves being "re-storied" in the building sense of that word. Instead of living in the sub-basement, we can move up to a twentieth-floor penthouse.

Put Music in Your Future

Ethel Waters was the daughter of a twelve-year-old unmarried girl. Ethel grew up in the slums and earned her first money by running errands for prostitutes. What happened to turn her life around so drastically? She had an encounter with Jesus Christ. She says that she was headed toward self-destruction when he changed her direction and her entire future. She became a world-class artist, who made popular the song that proclaims, "His eye is on the sparrow, and I know he watches me."

That kind of encounter has turned millions toward a new future as new creations. Pulling them out of their past slums, it put great music in their futures. How about you? Does your life feel like a condemned tenement? You don't have to settle for that. Moving into new quarters begins with a verb, *repent*.

Discovery Questions for Group Study

1. Do you agree with the contemporary trend of placing less emphasis on God's call for repentance and more emphasis on God's love and acceptance? Why?

2. Jesus said, "Repent, for the kingdom of heaven is at hand" (Matt. 3:2). What do you think that statement means today?

3. Some people think that if we truly love God as Jesus suggests in Mark 12:29-30, we have no need to repent. What do you think?

4. If sin in the singular sense (original sin) is the major problem we all face, is it really necessary for churches to mention the individual sins that result from that singular sin? Why?

5. Is the word *sin* outdated? List some other words you feel communicate the same meaning.

6. Have you known people who dramatically received the power of grace to make major life changes? What factors seemed to contribute most to their change of direction?

7. Among the several questions listed in the "To Be Specific" section, do you think any stand out as having particular relevance for Christians in your local community? In your congregation? In your denomination?

8. Distribute Bibles and study the passages listed with each "repent" sample from Jesus' teachings. What point did these words make to people in Jesus' day? What do these words say to you personally? What do these words say to contemporary Christians and to contemporary churches?

Chapter 2

FOLLOW: LEADERSHIP IS NOT ENOUGH!

The daughter applied for admission to an Ivy League university. Her father, filling out a questionnaire sent to him by the school, hesitated thoughtfully at the question, "Is she a leader?" Finally, he wrote, "I am not sure about this, but I know she is an excellent follower." A few days later, he received a letter from the president of the college. In it, the president wrote: "Our freshman group next fall is expected to contain several hundred leaders. We congratulate ourselves on the acceptance of your daughter as a member of the class. We shall thus be assured of having one good follower in the group."

Leadership has been promoted to a high status buzz word in contemporary society. Magazine articles suggest to managers of everything from dog pounds to multinational corporations that leadership is the way out of every present swamp. This faddish advice is accurate. Leadership determines the success of every business, institution, or human endeavor. Why, then, did Jesus so lightly emphasize the verb *lead*? Twenty times he said "Follow me." He used the word *lead* zero times. Why? Because leadership is not the first step in becoming an effective leader.

Someone described a certain bureaucrat as always quick to make a decision but seldom right. Willingness to move forward is an invaluable asset. But forward motion is a waste of energy, unless we are moving in the right direction. We cannot lead effectively without the right visions and values. Therefore, when Jesus began training a team of leaders to change the world, he focused on gathering the finest *followers* he could find.

Samples from Jesus' Teachings

As Jesus passed on from there, he saw a man called Matthew sitting at the tax office; and he said to him, "Follow me." And he rose and followed him. (Matthew 9:9; see also Mark 2:14 and Luke 5:27; 18:22)

Jesus said to him, "If you would be perfect, go, sell what you possess and give to the poor, and you will have treasure in heaven; and come, follow me." (Matthew 19:21; see also Mark 10:21 and Luke 18:22)

And Jesus said to them, "Follow me and I will make you become fishers of men." (Mark 1:17)

To another he said, "Follow me." But he said, "Lord, let me first go and bury my father." But he said to him, "Leave the dead to bury their own dead; but as for you, go and proclaim the kingdom of God." (Luke 9:59-60)

The next day Jesus decided to go to Galilee. And he found Philip and said to him, "Follow me." (John 1:43)

I am the light of the world; he who follows me will not walk in darkness, but will have the light of life. (John 8:12)

If any one serves me, he must follow me; and where I am, there shall my servant be also; if any one serves me, the Father will honor him. (John 12:26)

Speaking to Simon Peter in that last conversation on the seashore, Jesus said, "Follow me." (John 21:19)

[When Peter responded with jealousy toward another of the twelve, Jesus responded with] "What is that to you? Follow me!" (John 21:22)

Truly, I say to you, in the new world, when the Son of man shall sit on his glorious throne, you who have followed me will also sit on twelve thrones, judging the twelve tribes of Israel. (Matthew 19:28)

Related Verbs Jesus Used

Pennsylvania is called the Keystone State. Early settlers borrowed this nickname from the keystone in the center of stone arches, that ancient construction basic from which the word *architect* takes its root. Keystone accurately described a state whose borders are touched by five other states—more than any of the other thirteen colonies. *Follow* is a keystone verb in Jesus' speech. He uses at least twenty-two other verbs that mean the same thing or point in the same direction.

Come to me if you are heavy laden (Matthew 11:28) or hunger (John 6:35) or thirst (John 7:37-38; see also Matthew 23:37-38).

Abide in me like a branch in a tree (John 15:4-10).

Take my yoke upon you and learn from me (Matthew 11:29).

Love God with all your heart, soul, and mind (Matthew 22:37).

Seek first his kingdom and his righteousness (Matthew 6:33; Luke 12:31, 18:17).

Render to God what is his and to Caesar what is his (Matthew 22:21 and Mark 12:17).

Worship the Father in spirit and truth (John 4:23).

Do the will of God and you are part of my family (Mark 3:35).

Honor the Son and you are honoring the Father (John 5:23).

Believe that I and the Father are one (John 14:8-11; 10:37-38).

Continue in my word (John 8:31; Luke 6:46-49; Matthew 5:21-43).

Keep my commandments and you will abide in my love (John 15:10).

Keep my word and you will not see death (John 8:51).

Believe in me and you can do the works I do (John 14:12-14).

Believe in me and you will have eternal life (John 6:40; 47-51; 7:38; 8:24; 10:9, 26; 11:25-26; 12:25-26, 44-46; 14:1-7).

Eat my body and *drink* my blood (Matthew 26:26; Luke 22:14-20; John 6:53-64).

Receive those who I send and you are receiving me (John 13:20).

Wash one another's feet (John 12:14-16).

Take heed how you *hear* (Luke 8:18).

Take heed and *beware* of all covetousness (Luke 12:15-20; 16:10-13; 18:24-25; John 2:16).

Take heed lest you be weighed down with dissipation, drunkenness, and the cares of this life (Luke 21:34-36).

Deny yourself and *take up* your cross (Matthew 16:24; Luke 9:23), for you will *drink* from my cup of sacrifice (Mark 10:38-45).

Beware that no one leads you astray, toward following someone else (Mark 13:5-6, 21-23; Luke 21:8-9; Matthew 24:4-5, 13).

Take heed, watch, for you do not know when the end time will come (Mark 13:32-37) and when I will return (Matthew 24:4-5, 13).

Receive the Holy Spirit (John 20:22; Acts 1:5-8, 11:16).

A Call to Action

A group of United Methodist leaders gathered to discuss ways of reversing their denomination's numerical decline. In one of the addresses, Bishop W. T. Handy of St. Louis said, "Our main purpose is not simply to add numbers to our rolls but to fulfill the basic purpose of the Church: to make disciples of Jesus. Not admirers of Jesus. Not scholars of Jesus. But disciples—followers of Jesus the Christ."[1]

The bishop's words help correct a frequent misunderstanding. Unlike some other world religions, the Christian faith is not a list of principles; it is a relationship. That relationship begins with the verb *follow.* Jesus said to Levi, or Matthew, that day at his tax office, "Follow me" (Matt. 9:9). Levi could have responded with, "I think you are a great guy. I will organize a Jesus Fan Club here in Capernaum." But Jesus was asking for action, not admiration. In his teachings, faith is always more than cerebral; it is result*full.* Some protested that his actional call seemed unreasonable (Matt. 8:19-22; Luke 9:57-62), and some did not follow (Mark 10:17-22). But those who said yes left everything of their old lives behind, even family ties (Matt. 10:37; Luke 14:26).

An old bromide pictures a handsome, single minister saying to a pretty young member of the congregation, "The renovation work on the sanctuary is almost finished. You should see our beautiful new altar."

She replies, "Lead me to it." Christians who say yes Jesus' "follow me" show that kind of action oriented enthusiasm.

When missionary E. Stanley Jones conducted great mass meetings in the cities of India, he said that Jesus is God's total answer to humankind's total need. When someone accused him of being obsessed with such ideas, Jones replied, "I wish I were. It would be a magnificent obsession."[2]

When General William Booth, founder of the Salvation Army, was asked for the secret of his effective life, he said, "God has had all there was of me. There have been persons with greater brains than I, persons with greater opportunity . . . I made up my mind God should have all of William Booth there was."

A girl reportedly came up to Dwight L. Moody after one of his evangelistic meetings and said, "I felt that God was calling me to go to the mission field tonight."

Moody asked, "How did you reply to that?"

"No, Lord," she replied.

"*No* and *Lord* are words that never belong together," Moody said.

According to Jesus, he was right. For us to call Jesus "Lord" means that we have decided to follow him. We can say, "No, Jesus." But we cannot say, "No, Lord." The two words are incompatible.

An intense concentration on the right theological beliefs has value. What we believe is important. Yet, beliefs alone can be sterile Christianity, unreproductive. The history of great Christians is not so much a history of people who *believed* as it is a history of those who *followed*. Augustine rejected Christ's call for years. His prayer was, "O, God, make me pure, but not yet." He did not find real faith until he started praying like Isaiah, "Here am I! Send me" (Isa. 6:8).

The Corrective for Two-headed Thinking

Americans currently seem to think in two opposite directions at once. Opinion researcher Robert L. Cohen, member of a firm that makes an annual in-depth poll of Americans' opinions, says that people are seeking "something to believe in" and "an anchor" or identity with groups. "There is a hunger for allegiances, a new valuing of rituals. People are in conflict, questioning institutions and authority but wanting to be a part of something."[3]

How do we resolve these two opposites, a yearning for connectedness and a fear of commitment to fallible institutions and authority figures? The answer is found in the word *follow*—not just anyone or anything but someone who is utterly and eternally worth following. When we make that decision, we are doing what Levi did that day. We meet our own deepest need by saying yes to a unifying, powerful force outside ourselves.

In preparation for a concert, the musicians began filtering onto the stage, taking their seats. As some of them began to warm up, the air filled with unrelated noises. When the conductor appeared, the confusion suddenly ended. All eyes centered on the world-famous maestro. As he raised his baton, the miscellaneous notes began cooperating with one another. The instruments, now related to a dependable authority outside themselves, made beautiful music.

The unrelated and often conflicting parts of our lives keep us in chaos until we find a powerful unifying and directing force to lead us. That is why Jesus said, "Follow me." We find our way home to peace within and connected fellowship with others by perfecting our "followship."

To Be Specific

We can see the shape of discipleship in Levi's life. But what does the call to become a Christian mean in our generation?

For one thing, to follow means more than morality. Pastor Walter Richey wrote in his church newsletter about a fellow he admired very much. He wrote that his friend doesn't drink alcohol or use tobacco in any form. He does not patronize bars or strip joints. Richey does not recall his friend's ever resorting to profanity, blasphemy, or obscenities. He has never cheated anyone in a business deal. Richey concludes his article by revealing that he is describing his dog.

Following Christ is more than morality. It is not less than morality, for it certainly includes that. But we can be morally upright and stay selfishly at home in our private Capernaums. The most prominent example of someone's saying no to Jesus is that of a young man who had followed the Ten Commandments all his life (Mark 10:17-22). Jesus calls us to leave town and join him in a relationship of discipleship. Morality is not enough.

Second, to follow means more than church membership. On an average day, Americans buy more than eighty thousand pieces of clothing and accessories with little alligators embroidered on them.

This behavior is one of many ways we search for a positive identity. For some people, joining a church is done from the same motive. Churches are trying to give a great gift to people—the call to follow Christ. But as congregations (and entire denominations) grow older, they increasingly tend to encase that gift in several layers of beautiful organizational wrapping paper. How frequently their leaders then begin to confuse the wrapping paper with the gift.

The Amplified Bible paraphrases one of the earliest definitions of church membership as "More *and* more there were being added to the Lord those who believed—[that is,] those who acknowledged Jesus as their Savior and devoted themselves to Him, joined and gathered with them—crowds both of men and of women" (Acts 5:14). Following is more than church membership. It is not less than church membership, for it certainly includes that. But we can connect with a church without connecting with Christ. (You can plug an electric lamp into anything. You can plug it into the carpet or the sofa or the end table, but that does not light the bulb.) This is why Paul said to the Corinthian church, "No other foundation can any one lay than that which is laid, which is Jesus Christ" (I Cor. 3:11). Following is more than membership in the church; it is a daily relationship with the Lord of the Church.

Third, to follow means more than a deep involvement in church work. Lloyd Ogilvie notes how easily and often we are seduced by the secondary. "We can become so preoccupied with a busy life working for the Lord that our personal relationship with him becomes perfunctory rather than primary."[4] Following is more than church work. It is not less than church work, for it certainly includes that. But we can stay busy at Christian activities without staying connected with Christ.

Fourth, to follow means more than an accumulation of religious knowledge. If it were possible to lose weight by knowing about diets, most people would be slender. And if it were possible to tighten sagging muscles by reading about exercises, most people would be trim and fit. Stick to a diet? Most of us would rather talk about it! Exercise daily? Who has the time? Persons who develop high volumes of religious knowledge increasingly face the danger that their faith becomes knowledge centered rather than Christ centered. That can be one of the tragic results of a knowledge centered Christian education. It can cause the recipient of the knowledge to transfer unknowingly the focus of faith from Christ to a knowledge about Christ. When that happens, we fall into the same trap as the Jewish teacher, Nicodemus, to whom Jesus spoke late one night (John 3:1-21). We get filled with information and empty of a connection with the living Spirit of God, who makes the information worth having. Following is more than knowledge.

Being a follower leads to activity. Passive Christian followers do not exist. Making an exact list of what those followers do is not possible. The specific actions of each follower always grow out of his or her daily relationship with Christ—just as what a spouse should do for his or her marriage partner always develops from their interactive relationship. But the following questions surely belong on a list of Christian activity basics.

Do we follow Christ with our life-styles? A father and son were raking leaves when they noticed something darting in and out of the piles. After careful effort, they uncovered a chameleon. It was difficult to see among the brown leaves. It had blended with them by turning brown, too. After catching the little creature, they put it in a jar of green grass, where it immediately turned green. When they added some red berries, the chameleon began to take on that color. Some people are chameleons in character; wherever you put them, they turn that color. Their thinking and behavior depend on their environment.

Those who decide to walk with Christ are not granted immunity to social conformity pressures. To keep on following often means moving out of step with other people. That can bring risk and pain. Yet, holding on to the color of Christ in a stressful environment has its positive sides, too. Intelligent people find little satisfaction in marching with a band that is going in the wrong direction.

Do we follow Christ by seeking his will in life decisions? Sitting in his boat on a poor fishing day, a man on the California coast wondered why a small plane kept circling his boat. Suddenly, the pilot buzzed him dangerously low. Angry enough to throw the bait bucket at the plane, the fisherman sat up just as the pilot's handkerchief fluttered down a few yards away. Printed in crude letters was the message: "Do I have to bang you on the head? Large group of fish where I circle."

Seeing that the plane was now circling a spot about half a mile away, the fisherman started the motor and was soon under the plane. What a large school of prized white sea bass! It was his best fishing day ever!

When the Hebrews were traveling to the Promised Land, they received their manna (food) from God on a daily basis (Exod. 16:35). It did not come in advance; they had to go out and gather it daily. Jesus said that if we want the best gifts of God's Spirit we must seek, knock, and ask (Matt. 7:7). Too often, our egotistical desire to maintain the illusion of self-sufficiency blocks us from adopting that attitude. God may occasionally resort to banging us on the head, but he usually waits for us to turn our attention in his direction. If we never look his way, we end many of our days with empty stringers.

Do we follow Christ by staying connected with him through worship? Chaplain William G. Chrystal describes a night training flight in which he was a passenger. The plane made so many 360-degree turns that he became disoriented. The centrifugal force on his body gave some clues, but he suddenly became aware that he was seeing stars outside the plane's window at an angle where the ground should have been. Only by looking at the "artificial horizon" on the instrument panel could he be sure about what pilots call the airplane's "attitude" in relation to the earth.[5]

Jesus did not come just to give us eternal life; he came to give us abundant life on a moment-by-moment basis. Worship is one of the primary ways we can determine whether our attitudes coincide with the horizons of reality. When we regularly connect with Christ through the instrument panel of worship, we stay close to the possibility of life at its best. When we look away too much, we begin to have trouble distinguishing up from down.

Do we follow Christ by helping with his work in the church? A man said to his pastor over a cup of coffee one Monday morning, "I am really sore this morning. I played football all afternoon yesterday, played three full games." The pastor was puzzled for a moment, until he realized that his friend meant he had watched three football games on TV. Paul said that the Church is the body of Christ (Col. 1:24). This means that the Church is in the business of being and doing and saying what Christ was and did and said. That takes some organization, some planning, and some work—enough work to make people tired. We cannot accomplish that from the sideline or a reclining rocker. That takes more than the kind of prayer that says, "Use me, Oh Lord, in some advisory capacity!"

Do we follow Christ by using our energy and resources to help him fix what is broken in our world? Two weeks had passed since the boss hired Phil as a clerk. Phil was not doing well, so the boss called him in for a warning lecture.

"Young man, we have had people who were slow, but you are the slowest clerk I have ever seen. Aren't you quick at anything?"

The new employee thought a moment before responding with, "Nobody gets tired as quick as I do." Followers of Christ face a similar temptation.

Jesus performed a miracle by bringing Lazarus back to life (John 11:38-44). But before doing that he asked the disciples to remove the stone from the door of the tomb. After their doing that, he asked the disciples to strip away Lazarus' grave clothes. Jesus did not work alone then, and he does not work alone today. He asks his followers to exert energy. He does not do with miracles what his followers can do by their own talent and resources.

Do we follow Christ with the willingness to carry a cross? When Hitler began interfering with the churches and humiliating the German Jews, Dietrich Bonhoeffer, a loyal German himself, began to resist and protest. He refused to participate in the state churches, which bowed to the fuehrer's demands. Several of Bonhoeffer's colleagues urged him to bend. They argued that they would lose the opportunity to preach altogether if they followed Bonhoeffer's example. He replied, "One act of obedience is better than a hundred sermons." He eventually paid with his life for holding that conviction.

Fortunately, few contemporary Christians are asked to carry that kind of cross. Yet, in every instance where significant progress occurs in our world, someone has to carry a cross to make it happen. As the early Church was planted and began to take root in the Roman world, there was no gain without pain. The *status quo* are often "defective quo." And very often the only people who can delete these inferior status quos are those with the courage to carry a cross.

The Main Thing

An old Danish fable describes a spider that built its web in a barn. It started by spinning a long, thin thread and attaching it to a high beam. Knowing the thread was strong, the spider jumped off fearlessly. Spinning out more thread, it continued to descend. When it reached the spot where it knew the web should be, the spider began spinning out other threads, fastening them to the walls like the spokes of a wheel. Next, the spider spun a spiral thread, round and round, attaching it at each point where it crossed the spokes. "Now, I'll catch many flies," the spider said. "I will have plenty of food." Time passed. The spider grew affluent and self-satisfied. One day, months later, the spider was wandering around, cleaning its web. It saw a long, fine thread stretching upward toward the darkness of the roof. "I wonder what that is for," the spider said to itself. "It doesn't catch any flies. Why did I ever put it there?" And so, thinking it useless, the spider broke it, and the whole, wonderful web collapsed.

The most obvious parts of Christianity—the church oganization, the worship rituals, the theological beliefs—as important as they are, must not be confused with the main thing. Christian faith becomes strong and stays strong because of a single thread: our continuing, daily connection with Jesus as the Lord of life. When we cut that thread, we fall back into a dependence on ourselves, our wisdom, and our ability—and we fall into failure.

The famous Chapel of Loretto in Santa Fe, New Mexico, contains a twenty-foot-high stairway that winds into the choir loft. This engineering miracle, with no supports except its own form, has withstood several hundred years of use. As a pastor and his wife entered the chapel on their tourist excursion into Santa Fe, he paid little attention to the giant, life-size statue of Christ standing in a shadowy alcove on one wall. At a distance, it looked quite average. Shortly, however, the pastor felt a tug at his sleeve. "Go over there and stand right under that statue and look up into its eyes," his wife whispered. "It will give you the strangest feeling."

He obligingly wandered over, expecting nothing of significance. But the steel blue eyes looking down at him seemed so real that he waited breathlessly for the figure to speak and correct his lack of observational skills. This was the main thing in that room—not the elaborate stairway, but the Christ. That is also the main thing in every Christian life, and we stay connected to the main thing through the verb *follow*.

Discovery Questions for Group Study

1. In what ways is Jesus' call to "follow me" different for us than for the early disciples? In what ways is it similar?
2. From the section entitled "Related Verbs Jesus Used," assign a different verb to each member of the class. Ask each person to look up the text that goes with his or her related verb and then share with the group why they think the verbs are or are not related to the verb *follow*.
3. Is there really such a big difference between "believing in Christ" and "following Christ"? Have you known people who seemed to believe strongly but did not seem to follow? List some ways we can avoid that tendency.
4. Among the several questions listed in the "To Be Specific" section, do you think any stand out as having particular relevance for Christians in our local community? In our congregation? In our denomination?
5. Distribute Bibles and study the passages listed with each "follow" sample from Jesus' teachings. What point did these words make to people in Jesus' day? What do these words say to you personally? What do these words say to contemporary Christians and churches?

Chapter 3

PRAY:
WIRED FOR
ELECTRICITY?

Billy Sunday, the pro baseball player turned evangelist, was the Billy Graham of America's early 1900s. As part of his preparation, Sunday prayed for specific people in the city where he was going to conduct a campaign. Prior to the Columbus, Ohio, crusade, he wrote his customary letter to the mayor, requesting a list of the names of persons especially in need of prayer. The mayor responded by mailing him the city directory. One of Jesus' frequently used verbs expresses that same truth. Without exception, we all need to pray.

Our connection with God is a relationship, not a specific behavior. Yet, that relationship is sustained through a specific behavior—prayer. Like the electrical wiring in our homes, the practice of prayer carries the current. Remove that conduit, and you cut off the power. As Harry Emerson Fosdick said, "Failure in prayer is the loss of religion itself." Even though we involve ourselves in many other fine religious practices—church membership, church attendance, tithing, holding office—we stay distant from God without sincere, habitual prayer.

Auguste Sabatier, a French theologian of the last century, defined prayer as the essence of religion: "It is a commerce, a conscious willed relation. . . . Prayer is religion in act—that is to say, real religion."[1] Every renewal leader in church history echoes that conviction. John Wesley, like many others who changed the world for God and good, rose at 4:00 A.M. to spend a lengthy time in prayer. A letter he wrote to Ellen Gretton in 1782 characterizes his convictions: "Proceed with much prayer, and your way will be made plain."

American Airlines board chairman Robert Crandall says that the company would be helpless without its thirty-four-million-dollar computer operation buried beneath eight feet of reinforced steel and dirt in Tulsa, Oklahoma. One of the systems monitors more than 1,500 flights a day, while another fills seats as completely as possible, and a third handles reservations. Built to withstand earthquakes and tornadoes, the facility is stocked with sufficient power and provisions to keep the planes flying for three days.[2] People who wish to stay connected with God should likewise plant Jesus' verb *pray* deep into their daily behavior.

Samples from Jesus' Teachings

And whatever you ask in prayer, you will receive, if you have faith. (Matthew 21:22)

Again I say to you, if two of you agree on earth about anything they ask, it will be done for them by my Father in heaven. For where two or three are gathered in my name, there am I in the midst of them. (Matthew 18:19-20)

Therefore I tell you, whatever you ask in prayer, believe that you have received it, and it will be yours. (Mark 11:24)

If you ask anything in my name, I will do it. (John 14:14)

In Matthew 6:7-13, Jesus teaches the disciples a model prayer (see also Luke 11:2-4).
In John 17, Jesus prays for his disciples.
Matthew 6:6 says we should go into our closet to pray.
Luke 11:5-13 says God gives us what we ask for persistently.
Luke 6:28 says we should pray for our enemies.
Mark 11:25 says we should forgive when we pray.
Mark 14:38 says we should pray to gain strength over temptation.
Luke 22:39-46 describes Jesus in the Garden of Gethsemane, praying and instructing the disciples to pray for the strength to avoid entering into temptation.
Luke 21:36 says we should pray at the earth's end time for the strength to endure.
Mark 9:14-29 says that some healing comes only through prayer.
Luke 16:23-24 says that joy results from praying in Jesus' name.
Luke 15:16 says prayer enables us to achieve lasting positive results.

A Five-finger Exercise

Relating to God involves five kinds of communication: come to me; thank you; forgive me; help me; go with me. Memorizing these five can help Christians talk with God in the way Jesus taught his first disciples.

Come to Me. Scholars who have analyzed prayers from across the centuries traditionally call this first stage "adoration." This admission that we need God moves us beyond the attitude of self-sufficiency. The Old Testament puts it this way:

> O come, let us worship and bow
> down,
> let us kneel before the Lord, our
> Maker!
>
> (Psalm 95:6)

Jesus puts it this way:

> Our Father who art in heaven,
> Hallowed be thy name
>
> (Matthew 6:9).

The early Church put it this way: "In your hearts reverence Christ as Lord" (I Pet. 3:15).

In Mark Twain's classic *Huckleberry Finn,* Huck describes exactly how not to begin communicating with God: "Miss Watson she took me in the closet and prayed, but nothing come of it. She told me to pray every day, and whatever I asked for I would get it. But it warn't so. I tried it. Once I got a fish line, but no hooks . . . somehow I couldn't make it work." A relationship seldom amounts to much if our prime objective is to use the other person. God's presence, not his power, is the foundational ingredient on which the kind of prayer Jesus taught is constructed. If we build a relationship with God through habitually coming into his presence, we will experience his power. If we approach prayer as an effortless way of getting fishhooks, we usually go away as puzzled as Huck Finn.

Devout Moslems pray five times a day, using the Oriental habit of kneeling with their faces toward the Holy City. While this acknowledgment of the need for God's presence can become a meaningless ritual, it is based on eternal truth. People who say that they do not feel the presence of God in their lives are bringing a "guilty" indictment against themselves. Spouses who spend no time with each other lose their sense of relatedness. And there is no way to know God without spending time with him.

Thank you. Classical analysts of prayer call this thanksgiving. By admitting our self-insufficiency, our minds move another step beyond the constricting circle of self-reference. The Old Testament puts it this way:

> I will give thanks to the Lord with
>   my whole heart;
> I will tell of all thy wonderful
>   deeds.
>
> (Psalm 9:1)

Jesus shows this attitude of dependency on God's grace in every aspect of his life. Even as he illustrated his coming death to the disciples at their last meal together, "he took a cup, and when he had given thanks he gave it to them" (Matt. 26:27). The early Church put it this way, "Continue steadfastly in prayer, being watchful in it with thanksgiving" (Col. 4:2).

A Sunday school teacher asked her six-year-olds if they had anything specific to pray for during the class prayer time. Little Bethany raised her hand and said, "Let's pray for my dog, Chipper. His foot got caught in the door."

The teacher said, "Fine, we'll pray for Chipper. Does anyone else have anything to pray about?"

When no hands went up, Bethany spoke again. "Let's thank God that Chipper can run on three legs!"

Bethany was articulating a thoroughly biblical suggestion. The attitude of gratitude deepens our sense of relatedness to God. Unless we continually give thanks, we may unwittingly substitute the habit of begging for the habit of praying.

Forgive me. Classical analysts of prayer call this confession or contrition. This admission of self-imperfection gives us the power to forgive others their imperfections toward us. The Old Testament put it this way:

> Have mercy on me, O God,
>   according to thy steadfast love;
> according to thy abundant mercy
>   blot out my transgressions.
> (Psalm 51:1)

Jesus put it this way: "And forgive us our debts, As we also have forgiven our debtors" (Matt. 6:12). The early Church put it this way: "Let us then with confidence draw near to the throne of grace, that we may receive mercy and find grace to help in time of need" (Heb. 4:16).

Asking forgiveness does more than clear our guilt record; it helps scrape the attitude of perfectionist judgmentalism off the windshield of our mind. If we tend to think that God built us better than most other models, we have difficulty feeling and acting out forgiveness toward others. Confession, without damaging our necessary and appropriate self-confidence, helps balance it with the recognition that we are all subject to imperfection.

Others of us have the opposite kind of thinking pattern. We habitually put the gun of perfectionist judgmentalism to our own heads. Admitting our failures through regular confession helps combat our inclination to think that we ourselves cannot be forgiven by God and by others.

Help me. Classical analysts of prayer call this supplication or petition. With specific requests, we move even further beyond the idolatry of self-sufficiency to ask for help in accomplishing what we know we cannot do alone. The Old Testament puts it this way: "Give ear, O Lord, unto my prayer; hearken to my cry of supplication" (Ps. 86:6). Jesus put it this way: "Give us this day our daily bread" (Matt. 6:11). The early Church put it this way: "In everything by prayer and supplication with thanksgiving let your requests be made known to God" (Phil. 4:6).

Some people feel comfortable praying for big things, such as world

45

peace, but feel selfish praying for something personal, such as a pay raise. Jesus says that God is equally interested in large and small matters. In his model prayer, Jesus taught the disciples to pray for something as big as God's kingdom and as small as their daily bread. Trying to decide whether some prayers are selfish may cause us to miss a far more important issue in this subject. The most self-centered thing we can do is not to pray at all. Is that not a way of saying that we ourselves are God and don't need to talk with the real God?

Go with me. Classical analysts of prayer call this dedication. By this attitude, we ask God to help us accomplish future goals that are not just ours but his as well. The Old Testament puts it this way: "For with thee is the fountain of life; in thy light do we see light" (Ps. 36:9). Jesus put it this way "For thine is the kingdom, and the power, and the glory, for ever" (Matt. 6:13 KJV). The early Church put it this way: "We receive from him whatever we ask, because we keep his commandments and do what pleases him" (I John 3:22).

After her bedtime prayers, a little girl looked up and said, "And now, Lord, is there anything I can do for you?" All authentic prayers conclude that way. If our talking with God does not end on that note, we may need to ask whether it is a religious form of egocentric selfishness.

Spiritual giant E. Stanley Jones said that his call to the mission field followed his prayer that someone would respond to that need in an audience he was addressing. "Be careful how you pray," Jones warned. "You may be the answer."[3] This does not happen every time we pray. To think that God has no other way of getting things done except through us is religious egotism. But when we communicate with God about a need that is with his will, he often turns on a light in our own minds regarding how to meet it. If God never suggests any personal action to us at the end of our prayers, we should spend more time listening before we say amen.

Bottom Line Benefits

Prayer totals out to an infinite number of stupendous benefits in the ledger of daily life. The following list contains some of the most frequently reported positives.

Guidance. In one of Walt Kelly's "Pogo" comic strips, Pogo is sitting on a log as his friend Rabbit runs by. Pogo asks where he is going in such a rush. Rabbit says that he does not know, but he is responding to an emergency. "What's all the hurry if you don't know where you are going?" Pogo asks.

"Man, that's just it!" says Rabbit. "It's when you don't know where you is going that you gotta be in a hurry!"

Mahatma Gandhi, whose spiritual leadership brought India into the twentieth century, said that there is more to life than increasing its speed. Without the right sense of direction, how quickly we arrive does not matter. Prayer is one of the best maps for choosing the right highway.

After telling the mountaineer what to do in order to regain his health, the doctor said, "That'll be thirty dollars."

"For what?" growled the crusty patient.

"For my professional advice," replied the doctor.

"No, siree! Made up my mind not to take it," answered the patient as he walked out the door. When we fail to pray, we have made up our minds not to take the best advice available.

Courage. Several years ago, Bishop Fulton J. Sheen entered a New York hospital for open-heart surgery. A young priest who visited him the night before the operation was amazed at the bishop's lively attitude. Sheen quipped about current New York City happenings and inquired about church events, seeming to have forgotten why he was hospitalized.

"Bishop Sheen," the young priest finally interrupted, "You seem so calm. This is a very serious operation. Aren't you worried?"

"No," said the bishop. "You see, I'm all prayed up."

Jesus does not, however, suggest that prayer replace common sense. As his ship was sinking, the captain shouted through a megaphone to the crowd on the dock, "Does anyone know how to pray?" When a minister stepped forward, the captain said, "Wonderful. Start praying while the rest of us put on life vests. We are one short." Jesus neither used nor advised that kind of praying.

Power. The depth of Gandhi's teachings about prayer exceeded that of most Christians. "Prayer is not an old woman's idle amusement," he said. "Properly understood and applied, it is the most potent instrument of action" (*Non-Violence in Peace and War*). Life is filled with brick wall circumstances that neither genius nor talent is sufficient to penetrate. In some impossible situations, the passive power of prayer is the strongest force available. When Jesus healed people, he prayed for them. When he came to the toughest moment of his own life—the cross—he met it with the power of prayer.

Jesus does not, however, tell us to substitute prayer for intelligent action. The old story is close to being biblical when it quotes Deacon Jones as saying, "When I pray for a chicken, sometimes I get a chicken, and sometimes I don't. But when I pray for God to send me after a chicken, I always get a chicken."

Church Leadership Empowerment. The world's largest church—Yoido Full Gospel Church of Seoul, Korea—has grown to 520,000 from its starting size of five members in 1958. Professor of church growth C. Peter Wagner says that prayer, not academics or seminary training, seems to be the secret of the growth of this church. Along with the highly structured small groups that meet weekly, each member is required to spend a minimum of one hour each day in prayer. Pastor Paul Yonggi Cho said during an international conference, "God can only work when you let him out of the bottle. . . . Prayer moves the hand of God."[4]

That sounds similar to what another man named Paul wrote to the Ephesians. He says that God uses the same power to change human lives and build up the church that he used to raise Jesus from the tomb. The key to success in any church leadership role is to put our minds in the kind of attitude to receive that power. In other words, the most active thing we can do in church life is passive—to get people praying—so that the Spirit can come in power upon them and their goals.

An Arizona father found his small son trying to move a big boulder in the back yard. "Are you using all your strength?" the father asked.

"Yes, Daddy," the son replied.

"No, you are not," the father said. "You haven't asked me to help you." Church leaders who do not ask for additional help are not using all their strength.

Self-Discovery. In the crowded streets of Vienna, Austria, a tourist observed a blind person whose guide was describing the sights to him. What a tragedy it was, the tourist felt, to be in one of the great cultural centers of the world, with timeless statues and paintings by the great masters everywhere, and not be able to see them. But is life not like this for all of us? So much of our own greatest potentiality is invisible to us or perceived as through a glass darkly. That is another reason Jesus urges us to pray. Some of what we need to see can come to us only through the eyes of God.

Self-Improvement. Eighteenth-Century New England theologian Jonathan Edwards frequently berated Christians whose ideals failed to blossom into behavior. "Dull and lifeless wouldlings" he called these actionless thoughts. Prayer is one of the best ways to turn intentions into actions. People who regularly spend time in prayer often possess an observable depth and quiet reserve not seen in others. Prayer gives God an opportunity to redecorate our interiors.

Providence. One September Sunday morning in the early 1960s, the pastor of a Mattoon, Illinois, church invited the congregation to pray for rain. Lightning immediately struck a transformer near the church, and the service was continued by candlelight. Providence seldom comes so instantly, but as someone has said, "The more I pray, the more coincidences seem to happen in my life." We should amend that to say, "The more we pray, the *fewer* coincidences happen. The more of what God wants to happen, happens."

This does not mean that every accident is an act of God. Nor does the providence that so often follows prayer mean that God always gives people who pray what they want. Only the most thoughtless parent instantly gives a child everything he or she requests. God answers prayer, but sometimes the answer is no. In some instances, he knows that a refusal is the only way we can grow stronger. At other times, he can see further into the future than we can. Instead of giving us just anything, he wants to give us the right thing.

49

Ten Steps to God

In order to pray, we must first let go of our sense of self-sufficiency. Prayer is an admission of dependency of which many people are terribly frightened. This natural psychological barrier is compounded in persons whose human parents were dominating, undependable, or capricious. They desire intimacy with God, but they also fear it.

After they break through this barrier of dependency and fear, many people remain blocked at the question of how to begin. The following steps, used fifteen minutes each day, have enabled thousands of people to experience God's peace, joy, and power. The billfold-sized card from which they are taken is available in quantity from the Net Resource Center, 5001 Avenue N, Lubbock, Texas 79412.

As you begin this adventure, remember that prayer is an experience, not an idea. In some ways, prayer is like riding a bicycle; you learn only by doing it, never by thinking about doing it.

Commit yourself to following methodically these ten steps for fourteen consecutive days. Most people report that they do not as fully experience God's presence during their first three or four days as they do after several days of practice. Persist in your reaching out to God, and he will come to you. Like falling in love, the experience of God's presence is impossible to define. But when it happens, you will understand why great Christian leaders of every century have so enthusiastically recommended and practiced prayer. And you will understand what Jeremiah meant when he said, "You will seek me and find me; when you seek me with all your heart" (Jer. 29:13).

1) In preparation, set aside fifteen minutes in a location where you can be physically relaxed and there is little likelihood of interruption. Read one or two chapters from the Bible, listening for what God says to you. This helps to erase distracting thoughts from the blackboard of your mind. The following passages are especially helpful in preparing for prayer: John 14, Psalm 23, Matthew 5:1-12, Romans 8:35-39, I Corinthians 13, Psalm 91, Matthew 6, John 3:1-17, Psalm 46, Romans 12, John 15, Psalm 27, Psalm 103, Psalm 121, Isaiah 55, Luke 15, Psalm 84, John 1:1-18, Psalm 90, Psalm 19, I John 4:7-21, Psalm 139, Luke 24, Psalm 130, Luke 18:1-17.

2) Close your eyes and give thanks for three personal blessings of which you are especially conscious today. This helps you move toward God by moving away from a sense of your own self-sufficiency.

3) Ask God to help three other persons who you feel need his help today. Ask God to help your pastor(s). This helps you move toward God by moving away from self-centeredness.

4) Ask God to forgive your mistakes and sins and give you the strength to forgive others.

5) Ask God to help one person whom you find it hard to like. Ask God to give that person insights into his/her personal problems and ask God to give you the power to let his love flow through you to that person.

6) Ask that you will be sensitive to the needs of one person today whom God may want you to share his love with in word or deed.

7) Ask for insights into your personal problems.

8) Ask for help in achieving your personal goals.

9) Ask that God will tell you the most important thing you need to do today in order to "seek first his kingdom." (Matthew 6:33a)

10) Conclude by listening intently for three minutes to what God may say to you.

At dusk on a busy city street, a woman was trying to turn on the light in a phone booth so that she could read the directory. Seeing her frustration, a passerby said, "Lady, if you will shut the door, the light will come on!" If we want the best insights for healthy living, we must occasionally shut out the tension and distraction so that the light of God can come in.

Discovery Questions for Group Study

1. Do you agree or disagree with Harry Emerson Fosdick's statement that "failure in prayer is the loss of religion itself"? Why?

2. If our connection with God is a relationship rather than a behavior, does it matter how you behave? Why?

3. Assign one of the phrases from Jesus' model prayer in Matthew 6:7-13 to each member of the group. Give each person two

minutes to write out a paraphrase of his or her assigned phrase. (A paraphrase expresses the same meaning in different words.) Take turns reading the paraphrases aloud.

4. The "Five-finger Exercise" section of this chapter describes five kinds of prayer. Can you think of a type of prayer that could not be classified under one of those five categories?

5. After someone reads aloud the list from the section in this chapter entitled "Bottom Line Benefits," ask group members to name any other benefits not on this list.

6. Ask group members who have participated in a serious daily prayer discipline, such as that described at the end of this chapter, to share their experiences.

7. Distribute Bibles and study the passages listed with each "pray" sample from Jesus' teachings. What point did these words make to people in Jesus' day? What do these words say to you personally? What do these words say to contemporary Christians and to contemporary churches?

Chapter 4

BELIEVE:
PRAYER IS
ALMOST ENOUGH!

Each day of the year, an average of ten Americans die from accidental poisoning. More than one hundred million others poison their minds with negative thinking. In measuring how mental attitudes affect physical strength, a scientist used a gripping device that is squeezed with the right hand. The average grip of the experimental group was 101 pounds, but no one was told any results until the testing was over. By means of hypnosis, participants were told that they were very weak, and their average grip strength dropped to twenty-nine pounds. Still under hypnosis, the subjects were then told that they were very strong. Their average grip strength quickly rose to 142 pounds. When they *believed* they were strong, they were 40 percent stronger. When they believed they were weak, they became 79 percent weaker. The ideas we feed our minds are as important as what we feed our bodies. Negative thinking is the junk food of the brain. Positive belief makes a bigger difference than health food.

American showman P. T. Barnum was pointing toward that same life principle when he said, "More persons, on the whole, are humbugged by believing nothing, than by believing too much" (Ladies' Home Journal, [September, 1957]). Historian Philip Lee Ralph, in his book *The Story of Our Civilization*, put it this way: "When civilizations fail, it is almost always man who has failed—not in his body, not in his fundamental equipment and capacities, but in his will, spirit and mental habits. . . . Men—and civilizations—live by their beliefs and die when their beliefs pass over into doubt." John Wesley put it this way in a 1761 letter to a Miss March: "Keep close to your rule, the Word of God, and to your guide, the Spirit of God, and never be afraid of expecting too much."[1]

During the mid-1900s, many theologians developed an obsessive fear of emotional extremisms. Because that era was so strongly influenced by an emphasis on rationalism, they warned Christians against going too far beyond the logical, scientific, and historical evidence and believing too much about God. That may have been a valid danger during the revivalistic, overly emotional era of the early 1900s. Right now, however, our hazard seems to lie in the opposite direction—the danger of believing too little about God.

Paul Yonggi Cho recommends "positive confession," a type of prayer he calls "impossibility thinking," meaning that nothing is impossible for people who believe in God's ability to make a dream come true. That conviction seems very similar to the way Jesus used the verb *believe.*

Samples from Jesus' Teachings

All things are possible to him who believes. (Mark 9:23; see also Mark 9:17-29)

For truly, I say to you, if you have faith as a grain of mustard seed, you will say to this mountain, "Move from here to there," and it will move; and nothing will be impossible to you. (Matthew 17:20-21; see also Matthew 21:21, Mark 11:20-24, and Luke 17:5-6, 19)

And whatever you ask in prayer, you will receive, if you have faith (Matthew 21:22)

Do not fear, only believe. (Mark 5:36; for several illustration of physical healing through faith, see Mark 5:21-34, 35-36; Luke 18:42-42; John 11:40-44; Matthew 9:27-31)

Truly, truly, I say to you, he who believes has eternal life. I am the bread of life. (John 6:47-48)

God's Plus Sign

In New Testament usage, *believe* and *faith* are twins. We cannot discuss what *believe* means without understanding the meaning of the word *faith.* In its passive sense, faith can mean loyalty to a person or to a promise (as in "being faithful"). Or it can refer to the body of truth that constitutes the Christian message (as in "the faith which was once delivered to the saints" in Jude 3). In this chapter, faith is referred to in its active sense, meaning confidence in the words or assurances of another.

Whereas the Old Testament far more emphasizes good works as a way of relating to God, the New Testament emphasizes faith (Rom. 3:20-22). Even though the developmental history of the early church is called *Acts*, faith is the empowering basis for their actions. The first Christians called themselves believers (Acts 2:44). They tried to persuade others to believe in Jesus, in the truth of his teachings, and in his redemptive work on the cross. In the Old Testament, the words *faith* and *believe* appear only forty-seven times. In the New Testament, these two words appear almost three hundred times.

Halford Luccock once told the story of a little girl who reached that time in school when the mysteries of arithmetic began unfolding. She learned about the minus sign, the division sign, and the multiplication sign. As is always true when people learn something new, she began to notice things she had not seen before. One Sunday at church, she saw the large gold cross on the communion table. Beaming with excitement, she whispered, "Look, there is a big plus sign at the front of the church." She was more right than she knew. The cross is God's great plus sign, hung in the hallway of history. We cannot fully understand faith without the cross. It propels us toward four great beliefs by which God adds meaning and power to our lives.

Belief in God's Son. Christian faith is essentially different—not just in degree but also in genre—from self-help psychologizing. When we ask people to believe in Christ, we are not merely urging them to move toward a victory. We are bringing back the report of a victory that has already happened: the resurrection. This makes Christian faith quite different from other world religions. While we certainly wish to respect the views of other religions, any similarities to Christianity are minor when compared with the one major difference: an empty tomb. "Then they said to him, 'What must we do, to be doing the works of God?' Jesus answered them, 'This is the work of God, that you believe in him whom he has sent' " (John 6:28-29; see also John 20:29 and Mark 16:16).

Belief in God's Truth. Former Navy spy Jerry Whitworth was sentenced to 365 years in prison for his role in the Walker spy ring. The judge said Whitworth was not acting out of sympathy for the Soviets. Rather, he was a person who "did not believe in anything at all. He is the type of modern man whose highest expression lies in his amorality." Quaker philosopher Elton Trueblood described our society as a "cut-flower" civilization. The basic Christian truths have built it, but if we are disconnected from our roots, our ideals and ethics eventually fade and die. If we successfully give Christ to the next generation, we must hand his teachings to them, too. "Believe in the gospel" (Mark 1:15). "He who rejects me and does not receive my sayings has a judge . . . the Father who sent me has himself given me commandment what to say" (John 12:48-49).

Belief in God's Power. When Cabeza DeVaca wrote about his trip from Texas to the Pacific during 1530 to 1536, he described how the Indians insisted that he and his companion cure their sick. The Indians believed them to be gods, so they had to try. "We had to heal them or die, so we prayed for strength," DeVaca wrote. They were astonished, after laying their hands on and blessing the sick, that the people actually were healed. "We thought we had given away to doctors and priests our ability to heal. But here it was, still in our possession. . . . We were more than we thought we were."

An old story describes a man who went to buy a Rolls Royce. "It's the most famous car in the world," the salesman said. "Some Rollses are still running after fifty years." As the man was driving his purchase home, he realized that he had forgotten to find out how much horsepower the car had. When he went back to ask, the salesman couldn't find the answer anywhere in his materials, so he sent a wire to London, asking what the horsepower was. The telegram reply was one word—adequate. While few of us receive the power to heal the sick, what Jesus said is still accurate: "He who believes in me will also do the works that I do; and greater works than these will he do" (John 14:12).

When we undertake something for God that is within his will, we find the horsepower adequate.

Belief in God's Providence. A minister was called to the hospital late at night. In one room was a son who had been critically injured in an automobile accident. In another room was his father, who had experienced a heart attack when given the news about his son. Both were in serious condition. As the pastor met the wife and mother of the two, he expected to find her distraught. But she said calmly, "It's terrible, but I'm not going to come to any conclusions until God gets through with this. I don't know what he may yet do in spite of how bad things look."

Rational thinking is an essential element in decision making. It helps us to rely on what can be seen and measured. Faith, on the other hand, allows us to rely on what cannot be seen and measured. There is no substitute for that, either. Jo Layne Sumpter describes a takeoff from London's Heathrow Airport.

> The runway was wet, a light rain falling, and the sky was completely overcast. The plane started moving forward and we relaxed against the seats. Suddenly the plane started straight up through the clouds, and in a matter of minutes there was beautiful sunshine everywhere. . . . We had put our faith into the pilot, and the crew of the plane to take care of us and they did. . . . This is the kind of faith the Lord wants us to have.[2]

Jesus prayed in the garden that he would not have to drink the cup of pain, but he asked that God's will be done rather than his own (Matt. 26:39). Because he gave himself to God's providence, the resurrection occurred. The apostle Paul said, "O the depth of the riches and wisdom and knowledge of God! How unsearchable are his judgments and how inscrutable his ways!" (Rom. 11:33).

Overcoming Functional Atheism

A speaker at a business convention said, "God has already done for you what he is going to do for you. He has placed talents in you. Now, it is time for you to do your part and use them. It is like electricity. It is in your house, but you have to throw the switch." That view makes a positive motivational pitch for a sales meeting, but peel the rhetoric away and you have functional atheism—the belief that nothing happens unless we make it happen. Jesus said that God acts after our birth as well as before. He is a God *in history*, not a God of *prehistory* who now waits in a rocking chair to see how we will handle things. When Jesus urges us to believe, he is urging us to operate on the assumption that God is not asleep or in a coma. This conviction provides an antidote for three of life's most poisonous snake bites: fear, anxiety, and depression.

Fear. As he trains the disciples for a mission in which they will face the threat of death, Jesus says, "Fear not; you are of more value than many sparrows" (Luke 12:7; see also John 12:1-12). As he has dinner with them before going out to face his own death, he says, "Let not your hearts be troubled, neither let them be afraid" (John 14:27). As he prepares Paul for a life-threatening task, he says to him in a vision, "Do not be afraid, but speak and do not be silent; for I am with you, and no man shall attack you to harm you" (Acts 18:9-10).

Hindu nationalist leader Gandhi said, "Where there is fear, there is no religion." Scottish historian Thomas Carlyle declared, "We must get rid of fear; we cannot act at all till then. A man's . . . very thoughts are false . . . till he has got fear under his feet" (Heroes and Hero-Worship). By absorbing Jesus' advice to believe, the Christian giants of every age have arrived at that destination. On June 27, 1530, at the height of a hostile conflict, Martin Luther wrote his questioning colleague, Phillip Melancthon,

> Christ knows whether it comes from stupidity or the Spirit, but I for my part am not much troubled about our causes. Indeed, I am more hopeful than I expected to be. God who is able to raise the dead, is also able to uphold his cause when it is falling, or to raise it up again when it has fallen, or to move it forward when it is standing. If we are not worthy instruments to accomplish his purpose, he will find others. If we are not strengthened by his promises, where in all the world are the people to whom these promises apply?[3]

A Colorado Springs pastor, William E. Bowles, says, "Faith is to risk soaring like a glider out away from solid ground. Faith is finding the hidden laws of nature and supernature, ascending above the surface of living, risking the higher, broader, longer view of life." *Believe* is the verb that makes that possible. Yes, intelligence is a precious possession, but belief is sometimes much smarter.

Anxiety. "Therefore I tell you, do not be anxious about your life, what you shall eat, nor about your body, what you shall put on" (Luke 12:22; see also Luke 12:23-31). Twenty centuries after this was written, human feelings have not changed. A Gallup Poll survey shows that financial insecurity remains the chief worry for American families, with 56 percent citing this as their biggest personal concern.[4] What is the answer to this and the other kinds of anxiety that gnaw the joy out of living? Bill Gove was echoing Jesus' recommendation when he said, "The only way you can improve your life is to improve the quality of your perceptions."[5] Many people are faith dyslexic; they have trouble seeing things the way God sees them. Without the power to believe in God's power, they die many times before they die, of self-inflicted vision trouble.

People who ride bicycles say it is much easier to climb a hill in the dark than during daylight. At night, the cyclist can see but a few feet ahead. The short-range headlight gives the illusion that the road is either level or not steep. In the daytime, a rider can see the whole hill. Jesus several times warned against "tomorrow overload," the habit of pulling all our future bad possibilities into today's range of vision. He recommended the firm belief that God will be there to meet us in all those bad tomorrows.

Many young adult Christians now practice the biblical discipline of fasting. Taken from Jesus' forty days in the wilderness and Paul's admonition to the early Church (Luke 4:2 and Acts 14:23), they find it spiritually invigorating. Another kind of abstinence would do us even more good. We should renounce our consumption of anxiety and substitute a belief diet.

Depression. "Do you now believe? . . . In the world you have tribulation; but be of good cheer, I have overcome the world" (John 16:31, 33). Inhabitants of POW camps often develop an emaciated appearance as a result of food deprivation. People can also be held prisoner by their own insufficient beliefs. When that happens over a long period of time, the result—which becomes apparent in their faces and manner—is called depression. In recommending good cheer for Christians, Jesus does not promise that their believing will eliminate obstacles. He says their believing attitude will empower them to see through the prison bars to God's beyond. Paul puts it this way: "In all these things we are more than conquerors through him who loved us" (Rom. 8:37). What a magnificent difference this conviction makes in handling what life throws at us! While in prison awaiting trial, Paul penned a letter to the Philippians, in which he expressed more joyful feelings than in any of his other letters. Joy is the food God gives people who believe, in spite of their imprisonment by despairing circumstances.

Believe and Receive

In addition to providing an antidote for fear, anxiety, and depression, believing produces three practical positives.

Reality Reshaping. As exercise centers can reshape the contours of a human body, believing can reshape the reality of human experience. Belief can do more than change our attitudes regarding our experience; it can actually change our experience. Augustine in the fifth century said, "Faith is to believe what you do not yet see; the reward for this faith is to see what you believe." Jesus said the same thing. Believing faith can move impossible mountains, across the international date line into present reality. As Leslie Weatherhead put it, "Faith is rather the psychological frame of mind in which alone God can get near enough to man to do *His* work . . . faith . . . is the state of personality in which God can exert *His* power."[6] In believing, people become true children of God, made in his image, if not co-creators, then at least subcontractors in shaping new reality from impossible obstacles. Those who believe receive.

When Napoleon's armies swept across Europe, one of his generals was preparing to attack the little town of Feldkirch on the Austrian border. It was Easter, and the citizens gathered to decide whether to resist or surrender. The pastor of the church told the people that they had been counting on their own strength, and that would fail. This was the day of the Lord's resurrection. He decided to ring the bells and have service as usual and leave the matter in God's hands. Napoleon's army misunderstood the meaning of the joyful bells. Assuming that the bells announced the arrival of the Austrian army, Napoleon's army broke camp and retreated. Believers do not always receive in such dramatic ways, but Jesus was right: God moves with those who move in his direction.

Peace. A pastor driving in a strange part of town passed a sign that read: "Paragon Place Motel." Impressed by the name, he later looked up the word paragon in the dictionary. It was "a model of excellence or perfection," according to Webster. Can we ever arrive, even for an overnight stay, at a "paragon place" in life? Are we not always in some form of stress? Is not life by definition an imperfect trip? Yet, those who believe arrive at a far more peaceful state of mind than those who don't. Believers come much closer to a paragon place than those who cannot believe.

In the days when cross-country travel was done mostly by train, a little girl accompanied her parents on a long trip. As they crossed their first river, she watched with wide-eyed fear. As they approached the next one, she said, "I'm scared we will run into the water." Then, she felt the train rattle onto the bridge. After the same thing happened twice more, she settled back and relaxed. "Somebody has put bridges for us all the way," she said. Those who believe receive many things. One of those things is peace.

Hope. Americans want to believe that their lives can be different in the future. This yearning is one of the major reasons why shopping centers fill up on Sunday afternoons. People hope life can be different by their buying something. But purchases provide only a temporary feeling "high." They can change neither our futures nor the permanent way we think about our futures. That only happens when we believe in a God bigger than materialism.

The Queen in Lewis Carroll's *Alice in Wonderland*, says, "It is a poor sort of memory that only works backwards." What Christians believe empowers them to remember the future with hope. Paul wrote to the church in Rome: "May the God of hope fill you with all joy and peace in believing, so that by the power of the Holy Spirit you may abound in hope" (Rom. 15:13). This is no Pollyana suggestion that we become more optimistic or more self-confident or that we practice positive thinking. Believing in God's power generates a psychological climate of faith in which hope grows as naturally as cotton in Mississippi. Paul does not urge Christians to work harder at feeling hopeful; he says they receive it as a gift.

Review the Bible's heroes and heroines. You find them, without exception, to be people of hope. Abraham set out from his home in Ur of the Chaldees, hoping for a promised land he had never seen (Gen. 12:1-4). When Moses set out from Egypt leading a band of ex-slaves, he had a prayer in his heart and hope in his head (Exod. 14). Joshua and Caleb returned from their spy mission in foreign territory, saying, "We are well able to overcome it" (Num. 13:30). The other ten scouts made the same reconnaissance tour and said the opposite: "We seemed to ourselves like grasshoppers, and so we seemed to them" (Num. 13:33). Isaiah and his refugees left Babylon for Jerusalem to face a shaky set of circumstances—a country in shambles, a temple destroyed, a government in ruins. Yet, Isaiah, chapters 40 through 55, are full of hope. They describe a future in which the refugees will mount up with wings like eagles and will walk and not faint (Isa. 40:31).

If you believe in God who loves you and empowers your future, you receive hope. You know that your present painful circumstances are only temporary. No matter how knotty your problems, God can untie them. Whatever sentence you are living out has an exclamation point at the end, not twenty dreary lines followed by a series of question marks. That is what kept Paul going through all those shipwrecks and floggings—not confidence in his own strength, but a hope born of believing in a power beyond himself. Paul did not say, "I can do all things." He said, "I can do all things in him who strengthens me" (Phil. 4:13). That statement of believing faith leads to genuine, lasting hope.

One Easter morning, a shabbily dressed flower lady was seated in her usual spot on a city street. Seeing the smile on her wrinkled face, a passerby said, "You look happy this morning."

"Why not?" she replied. "Everything is wonderful."

"Don't you have any troubles?" the man asked.

"You bet," she said. "But it's like Jesus and Good Friday. When I get to dwelling on my troubles, I try to remember what happened three days later: the Resurrection. So I cut God some slack. If I give him a chance, he usually fixes things in three days."

What is the best thing to give up for Lent? Hopelessness! But we cannot give that up unless we take up the belief that produces the state of faith that produces the opposite of hopelessness.

Too Soon to Tell

Floyd Legler, one of the people to whom this book is dedicated, went broke in the trucking business the first time he entered it. One afternoon during that period, he was sitting in a friend's kitchen eating cookies and milk—and glad to get them because he had no money in his pocket for lunch. The old friend said, "Floyd, aren't you sorry you went into the trucking business?"

Floyd thought a moment and replied, "It's too early to tell." A few years later, he was back in the trucking business and grossing eighteen million dollars annually. Too much of the time, we are not willing to wait for God to move in our situation. Christians believe that until all their innings have been played, it is too soon to tell.

John Claypool tells of driving into a village high in the Swiss Alps one afternoon and seeing a larger-than-life statue of an Alpine mountain guide on the outskirts. The statue wore the traditional pointed hat with a proud feather sticking up. A rope coiled over his shoulder, and his feet were encased in hobnail boots. His head was thrown back over his shoulder as if he were calling to others behind him. His finger pointed to the highest peak on the horizon. On the base of the statue was the inscription "Follow me." Claypool says that this is how Jesus offers to relate to us in terms of our future. This begins with the verb *believe*. Prayer is almost enough, but not quite. We pray, believing.

Discovery Questions for Group Study

1. Someone said that believing too much is irrational and believing too little is unchristian. Which of these do you think is the greatest tendency in contemporary Christian thinking?

2. Jesus said, "All things are possible to him who believes" (Mark 9:23). Do you think that statement applied only to the early apostles, or does it still have meaning today?
3. Do you believe in the "providence of God" discussed in this chapter? If so, how do you think it works?
4. Fear and anxiety can take us so far away from God that we become functional atheists. Does this mean that fear and anxiety have no value in our lives?
5. Break into groups of three to four people for five minutes. Ask each person to share some of the methods she or he has found helpful in coping with fear, anxiety, or depression.
6. Some people seem to be naturally inclined toward hopefulness about the future. Others seem naturally predisposed toward gloominess. Is there anything we can do to reshape these natural inclinations?
7. Distribute Bibles and study the passages listed with each "believe" sample from Jesus' teachings. What point did these words make to people in Jesus' day? What do these words mean to you personally? What do these words say to contemporary Christians and to contemporary churches?

PART II

How to Treat Other People

Chapter 5

LOVE:
GOD WITH SKIN ON

Long after going to bed, the three-year-old was whining and crying. Deciding that she would not give up and go to sleep, her father went in to ask what was wrong. "I'm scared of the dark," she sobbed.

"But you know there is nothing that will hurt you here in your room. And besides, God is right here with you to protect you," her father replied.

"But God doesn't have any skin on!" she retorted.

Christ was God with skin on. Through our connection with Christ, God empowers us to become God with skin on to other people. That life-powering process is summarized in one of Jesus' great verbs, *love*.

People who wear glasses do not have the power of good vision within themselves. Their lenses give them that power. Without a connection with God, loving other people unselfishly is like trying to read the paper without glasses. Although possible, it is difficult, it feels unnatural, and it works only for short periods. We must not, therefore, approach Jesus' instructions regarding love as great "oughts" or "shoulds." They are great "cans." When we choose to relate to God, he empowers us to live these verbs in the same way that lenses facilitate seeing.

Samples from Jesus' Teachings

You shall love your neighbor as yourself. (Matthew 22:39; see also Matthew 19:19 and Mark 12:31 Jesus illustrates what he means by loving your neighbor in the story of the good Samaritan [in Luke 10:25-37]).

A new commandment I give to you, that you love one another; even as I have loved you, that you also love one another. By this all men will know that you are my disciples, if you have love for one another. (John 13:34-35; see also John 15:12, 17.)

If you love me, you will keep my commandments. (John 14:15)

Related Verbs Jesus Used

Do not judge (Matthew 7:1; Luke 6:37, 41-42).
Give (Matthew 19:21; Mark 4:24, 10:21; Luke 6:30, 38; Acts 20:35).
Honor (Matthew 19:19; Mark 10:19; Luke 18:20).
If your brother sins, go tell him (Matthew 18:15-17).
Whoever divorces (Matthew 19:9, 18; Mark 10:11-12, 19; Luke 16:18; 18:20).
Do not kill (Matthew 19:18; Mark 10:19, Luke 18:20).
Do not steal (Matthew 19:18; Mark 10:19; Luke 18:20).
Do not tell untruths (Matthew 19:18; Mark 10:19; Luke 18:20).
Do not defraud (Mark 10:19).
Be merciful (Luke 6:27-36).
Humble yourself (Luke 18:14).

The Most Dependable Self-Help

An ancient clay tablet inscribed about 4000 B.C. tells of a mystic who believed that the secret of life could be discovered by going without food. Just as he was learning to live without food, he died. Those who attempt to live without love meet the same fate. When we reach out in love to other people, our self-esteem increases. When we concentrate on loving ourselves, it starves. Psychoanalyst Sigmund Freud eventually limited his treatment goals to two: bringing patients to the point where they could both work for a living and learn to love. "Work and love—these are the basics," he said. Theodor Reik wrote that without the capacity to love there is neurosis. Another prominent analyst, Erich Fromm, put it this way in his book *Man for Himself*: "To spare oneself from grief at all cost can be achieved only at the price of total detachment, which excludes the ability to experience happiness."

The sages of the ages have echoed those sentiments. In the fourth century B.C., Plato said in his *Symposium*, "He whom love touches not walks in darkness." Alfred, Lord Tennyson wrote in *Becket*, "Love is the only gold." Shelley said in "Alastor," "Those who love not their fellow beings live unfruitful lives, and prepare for their old age a miserable grave." American poet Archibald Macleish said, "What love does is to arm. It arms the worth of life in spite of life."[6] Why does the love section contain the largest number of pages in most quotation books? Because love is one of our greatest needs and one of life's most obvious truths. At the deepest level of our beings, we know that we get what we give. We would like to learn how to give more.

The Best Medicine for Others

"I have been practicing medicine for over thirty years," a physician said. "I have prescribed many things. But in the long run, I have learned that for most of what ails the human creature, the best medicine is love."

"What if that doesn't work?" the woman to whom he was talking asked.

"Double the dose," he replied.

J. Kenneth Kimberlin tells about a nurse in Sweden who started working in a government convalescent home. She was assigned to an elderly woman patient who had not spoken a single word in three years. The other nurses disliked this patient and always passed her off on the newest nurse. The new nurse decided to try unlimited love with this patient. She sat down in a rocking chair beside the one in which the patient rocked all day and just loved her. On the third day, the patient opened her eyes and said, "You're so kind." Two weeks later, she was well enough to leave the home.[2]

Madame de Staël was right when she wrote, "We cease to love ourselves if no one loves us" (*Portraits des femmes*). And pastoral counselor John Drakeford was right: "By people we are broken, and by people we are put together again." Love is not just a characteristic of our Creator; it is also our personal creator and recreator.

A pediatrician prescribes an unusual treatment for newborn babies who do not gain weight as they should. On the baby's chart the doctor invariably writes: "This baby to be loved every three hours." In order to remain healthy, humans of every age need this universal medicine. Love does not actually cure the many illnesses that result from insecurity, loneliness, or rejection. But it can make us want to get well. Love does not change the problems we face, but it makes us so strong that we can handle the problems.

Who Does Christ Tell Us to Love?

Christians receive power to love six categories of people. These are the same six groups we are most frequently tempted not to love.

Do we love our neighbors? A Roper Organization survey asked a random sampling of Americans to define success. The top four on a list of fourteen qualities Americans believe necessary in order to be successful involve positive relationships with other people.[3] In spite of that recognition, Jesus' admonition to us to love our neighbors continues to be among our toughest challenges.

A college student, riding her bike home from the University of Oregon in Eugene, was struck from behind by a car. Thrown to the roadside, her leg fractured, she lay helpless while numerous drivers slowed to look but did not stop. Fifteen minutes passed before a grocery store clerk saw her through the window and came to her aid.[4] This kind of story is now so familiar that psychologists refer to the behavior as the "unresponsive bystander phenomenon."

The greatest number and most damaging of such behaviors do not, however, involve distant neighbors but near neighbors. The pain of people who work at our elbow or in our office is as likely to be neglected as that of persons like Kitty Genovese, who was murdered in Queens, New York, in 1963 while more than thirty people watched. Our intense self-absorption inclines us to break Jesus' commandment without awareness. Experimental psychology studies of mice crowded together confirm what we observe in human society: The closer we live together, the more withdrawn into our own cocoons we often become.

One of the reasons for low-volume neighborly love is the natural difficulty we have in feeling the pain of others unless we have felt that same kind of pain ourselves. A minister who has spent many hours in hospitals with anguished relatives of patients says,

> The intensive care waiting room is a different world. No one is a stranger. They help one another. They grieve with one another and shed tears of joy together. There is no distinction of race or class. Vanity and pretense vanish. Everything focuses on the next doctor's report or that next telephone call. Here in this anxious stillness it becomes clear that loving someone else is what life is all about. Why does it take the intensive care waiting room to teach us to forget our irritations and love one another?

The answer, of course, is that we can feel best the pain in others that we have felt in ourselves. This explains the success of the dozens of self-help groups now being formed. Based on the pioneering model of Alcoholics Anonymous, we now have groups for the widowed, the divorced, single parents, the overweight, the lonely, and there are countless specialized groups for persons who suffer from life-damaging diseases. These "specialized Samaritans" are among the best answers to lack of love in crowded societies.

Do we love our enemies? So far in this century, our world has seen 207 wars. The two world wars took fifty million lives at a cost of $337 billion for World War I and $1.15 trillion for World War II. During 1986, more than forty wars were being waged. Why?

Bertrand Russell said, "Few people can be happy unless they hate some other person, nation, or creed." Those words express a truth upon which Hitler and every other despot recruited the energies of the masses to help expand their empires. And yet, there is an opposite truth, too: The more we express love toward other people, the more wholeness we feel within ourselves. This is a great paradox—our compulsive attempts to feel better about ourselves by hating someone and our need to feel better about ourselves by loving them. Jesus was not naive about human nature. He knew that even Christians would have enemies (people who bug us and get in the way of our comforts and our goals) and would feel inclined to hate those enemies. He said that we must decide (even when we do not feel like it) to resolve the paradox by taking intentional, specific, loving actions toward those persons—even if they do not deserve it.

In his newsletter *Context*, Martin Marty retells a parable.

> A holy man was engaged in his morning meditation under a tree whose roots stretched out over the riverbank. During his meditation he noticed that the river was rising, and a scorpion caught in the roots was about to drown. He crawled out on the roots and reached down to free the scorpion, but every time he did so, the scorpion struck back at him.
>
> An observer came along and said to the holy man, "Don't you know that's a scorpion, and it's in the nature of a scorpion to want to sting?"
>
> To which the holy man replied, "That may well be, but it is my nature to save, and must I change my nature because the scorpion does not change its nature?"

Jesus said the same.

Do we love other church members? "Love one another with brotherly affection; outdo one another in showing honor," Paul wrote the Romans (Rom. 12:10). "And may the Lord make you increase and abound in love to one another," he wrote to the Thessalonians (I Thess. 3:12). His need to give this advice infers that the Romans and the Thessalonians insufficiently practiced it. That sparsity has continued. About 1140, Peter, Abbot of Cluny, wrote these words to Father Bernard, "You perform all the difficult religious duties: you fast, you watch, you suffer; but you will not endure the easy ones—you do not love."

A new congregation in Lubbock, Texas, grew from 30 to 625 members in its first twelve months. When asked for the secret of this rapid growth, the pastor said, "The main thing I'm trying to do is build on care and prayer. . . . We view every person as a potential care minister." The church has fourteen care groups, which meet twice monthly.[5] All our failures in working with other Christians boil down to one residue: failure to love. When a church becomes an extended family—willing to laugh, cry, and celebrate with us, willing to be a crutch when we need support and a springboard when we need encouragement—it meets one of our most basic needs. Such churches grow both numerically and qualitatively.

Do we love our family? A pastor told of visiting some people who spoke in glowing terms about their neighbor, who was at that time a member of the pastor's church. They talked at length about what a great neighbor and friend this man was. And yet, the pastor knew that this wonderful neighbor hated his brother and sister. He hated them because of their appearance, the decisions they made, and for the things they did to him when they were children. It is often easier to make friends with your neighbor than with your own family.

The 1985 revenues for marriages in New York City totaled $779,420. The total revenues for annulments and divorces were $3,690,750. That is a statistical picture of the gap between our desire to love and be loved and our failure to achieve it. Someone said, "It is a good thing love is blind; otherwise it would see too much." Within two or three years, marital love inevitably begins to see too much. Unless romantic and sexual love are energized with Christian love, they have trouble surviving the view.

Do we love the lonely? An old story reports the conversation between a psychiatrist and a man who was unhappy about being discharged following years of analysis. "You're cured," said the doctor.

"Some cure!" the man snorted. "When I first came here, I was Napoleon Bonaparte. Now I'm nobody."

The world is filled with lonely people who feel saturated with the despair of nothingness and unconnectedness. In his book *The Snow Goose,* Paul Gallico tells the story of a lonely man whose heart was full of love but whose body was crippled. A hunchback, his left arm hung useless at his side. Gallico says that the man had mastered his physical handicap but was driven into seclusion by a failure to find anywhere a return of the warmth that flowed from him.

Our world contains countless such people. They extend love. They want friends. Yet, day after day the warmth they send out comes back stamped "addressee unknown." Sometimes this is an older person trapped in the isolation of age or illness. But just as often it is a youth (their lonely pain illustrated by the high teenage suicide rate). Crowds are not enough. Without someone who understands and accepts us, a stadium full of people is as lonely as a tomb.

Several years ago, a retail store employee in an Eastern city sent a money order to one of the company's branches in San Francisco. She asked for as many articles as it would buy to be sent to her as Christmas gifts from an anonymous friend. Her letter circulated through nineteen branch offices, producing an enormous deluge of anonymous gifts. There is a better cure for this kind of pain: one close-by Christian who is sensitive enough to see the loneliness and compassionate enough to care.

Do you love those outside our social and ethnic class? As E. Stanley Jones began his work among the low castes and outcasts of India, he said, "The way of Jesus should be—but often isn't—the way of Christianity. Western civilization is only partly Christianized." Michael Cassidy, speaking of the South African system of Apartheid, calls Christians, both white and black, to repent of their sins of racism and retaliation, and to approach one another for the purpose of genuine reconciliation.[6] The work Jones began in India and King continued in America is not yet finished.

How Does Christ Tell Us To Love?

Christians receive the power to express love to others in seven specific ways. These are the same seven ways in which they are most frequently tempted not to love.

Does our love move beyond thinking into action? While traveling in Africa, Robert Bell and his group drove far into the bush country to visit a chief and his family. Bell said that he was especially touched by the chief because he instantly saw through the façade of the visit. He asked them "Did you come to help or just to take pictures?"

Christians sometimes translate "love you neighbor" into "think positive thoughts about your neighbor." Avoid doing damage. Don't steal a lawnmower or sleep with his or her spouse. But love in the Christian sense is more than a passive thought or a withholding of harm. When Jesus used the verb *love*, he meant, "help your neighbors," reach out and do them some positive good that they can feel. Jesus was, himself, the model for this verb. God did more than simply refrain from doing us damage. He *sent* his Son. He actively sought us and sought to do us good. Matthew 14:14 captures Jesus' lifestyle: "As he went ashore he saw a great throng; and he had compassion on them and healed their sick." For those who chose to follow him, love is more than an attitude or a warm feeling. In addition to having brain cells, love has hands and feet. Christians do more than just take mental pictures of what happens around them; they take action.

Does our love move beyond the masses to individuals? There is a legend in which the devil was walking down the street with a friend. They noticed a man ahead, stooping to pick up something. "What did that man pick up?" the devil's friend asked.

"A piece of the truth," the devil replied.

"That is bad for your business," said the friend.

"Not at all," said the devil. "I am going to encourage him to organize it."

The newest interest among Christians in political and social action in recent years has produced many positive benefits. Yet, it brings a danger, too—the inclination to think of love only as a mass matter rather than an individual matter. Dostoevsky said in *The Idiot,* "In abstract love of humanity one almost always loves only oneself." Joan Baez was speaking for a great many of us when she said, "The easiest kind of relationship for me is with ten thousand people. The hardest is with one." God's children can look and act beautiful in the plural. In the singular, many of them are barely presentable and tremendously hard to love.

Ralph W. Sockman used to tell about a conversation Julia Ward Howe had one day with the distinguished senator from Massachusetts. She asked him to take a hand in the case of a person who needed some help. The senator answered, "Julia, I've become so busy I can no longer concern myself with individuals."

Julia replied, "That is quite remarkable. Even God hasn't reached that stage yet."

Does our love move beyond talking to listening? Mark Rutherford said that he would like to add one more beatitude to the list in the Gospels: "Blessed are they who heal us of self-despisings." That precious service comes mostly through listening. Nearly all educational institutions offer a course in public speaking. Yet, none of them offers one in public listening. If they did, we might have more skill, and the world might have less pain.

A Southwestern pastor reports a fairly common occurrence among ministers. Late one night a man called, refusing to give his name. He said that he planned to kill himself, but he wanted to talk with someone first. The pastor tried to talk him out of it—even offered to meet him—but the man hung up. The next morning's paper carried no suicide reports, so the man apparently had reversed his plans. To talk to someone is what most people need far more than they need to escape their problems—just to talk with someone who listens and cares.

Do we love enough to refrain from blaming? A sign at the entrance to the San Diego Zoo says, "Please do not annoy, torment, pester, plague, molest, worry, badger, harry, harass, heckle, persecute, irk, bully, rag, vex, disquiet, grate, beset, bother, tease, nettle, tantalize, or ruffle the animals." Many people would like to hang that sign at the entrance to their lives. The people who love them keep trying to improve them by blaming them, not knowing that a thimbleful of affirmation usually does more good than a truckload of blame.

"It's his fault. It's her fault. It's their fault. It's your fault." That kind of habitual speech pattern is usually a way of saying, "It's not my fault." That inclination to protect ourselves by pointing a finger elsewhere, first reported in the Garden of Eden story, is one of the most dependable genetic predispositions. Christians, because they know that Christ loves them enough to withhold blame, strive for a cease-fire. They know that love is not just listening. It also involves what we say—and do not say.

Do we continue to love, even when we do not approve of another's behavior? Another basic reflex is our tendency to lavish love when we are pleased with another's behavior and to withhold love when we are displeased with it. Quaker leader Charles Mylander reminds us that Christians are urged to keep love and approval in separate compartments, refusing to link them with one another. He says that love is unconditional, that we owe all people love, even if we disapprove of their actions. Approval, on the other hand, is conditional. It relates to how people act.[7]

Another pastor who has distinguished himself as a master in handling sharp differences of opinion in church and community life says that if we are to be effective in helping people change their ways, we must give "tons of continuous, unconditional love," while at the same time expressing disapproval about a particular behavior. Jesus gives the same prescription in Matthew 18:15-17. Christians, whether they approve or disapprove of a behavior, keep on loving. They know that few things get better without it, and most things get better with it.

Do we love enough to confront? In what sounds like a mythical story, the daughter of an educational psychology expert had become a continual discipline problem. One morning at breakfast she pushed her cereal away, announcing that she did not like that kind of breakfast. "Well, darling, what would you like?" the father asked.

"I want a worm," she whimpered.

Daddy went to the garden, got a fat worm, washed it, and laid it on her plate. "But I want it cooked!" she sobbed.

After the worm was rolled in butter and fried, she demanded, "I want Daddy to have half!" So Daddy dutifully divided the fried worm and managed to get his portion down.

This time, it was howls and sobs. "But that was the part I wanted," she said.

Love does not mean that we give our children—or anyone else—everything they want or do everything they ask us to do. Genuine love is sometimes tough enough to keep on loving while at the same time firmly saying, "No way! That is wrong. That will hurt you, me, or someone else. That is a road down which I will not walk."

Do we love enough to refrain from dominating? When a flood in Oklahoma drove many residents from their homes, several citizens provided emergency lodging. One woman went to live with a minister and his wife for several days. After a couple of weeks, she said to a friend, "I appreciate those people giving me a place to live, but I don't think I can stand to stay there much longer. That lady tries to run my life. She makes all kinds of decisions about how I need to fix up my house. She instructs me about how to talk with the Federal Disaster Center. I don't like it. But I feel obligated because they have given me a place in their home."

Two situations smother love's intended results: a loving but dominating mother or father and a merciful but dominating care-giver. Christians avoid stepping across the dotted line between compassion and controlling, between caring and conquering.

The Best Monument

Pastor David McKay describes his feelings while standing under a pine tree in the quiet of a cemetery in Des Moines, Iowa.

> As I stood there, I remembered the man who was not only my father, but who was also my minister! The man who shared his life totally and completely with anyone who asked!
> Charles Merrill Smith in a book he wrote, tells of the money raised, the buildings built, meetings attended, and all the rest which make an impression on the "higher ups." Then he says, "In the final assessment of a minister's life, the only real monument he leaves is the touch left upon another human life!" That is true, not only of a minister, but for all of us![8]

Discovery Questions for Group Study

1. Jesus said, "You shall love your neighbor as yourself" (Matt. 22:39). Make as long as list as you can of what "love your neighbor" means in contemporary life. Are some of these more important than others?
2. Jesus tells the disciples to love one another (John 13:34-35). List some of the ways in which your congregation lives out that suggestion. Are there ways by which you could do this even better?
3. Among the several questions listed in the "Whom Does Christ Tell Us to Love?" section, do you think any stand out as having particular relevance for Christians in your local community? In your congregation? In your denomination?
4. Distribute Bibles and study the passages listed with each of the related verbs Jesus used. What point did these words make to people in Jesus' day? What do these words say to you personally? What do these words say to contemporary Christians and contemporary churches?

Chapter 6

FORGIVE:
THE ULTIMATE
CHARACTER TEST

Clara Barton, founder of the nursing profession, was known as a person who never held resentments. When a friend reminded her one day of cruelty someone did to her several years previously, Clara seemed not to remember the incident. Amazed, the friend said, "You mean you don't remember the wrong done to you?"

"No," Clara answered. "I distinctly remember forgetting that."

While few achieve that level of saintliness, the story captures the essence of another of Jesus' great verbs: *forgive*. In the mind of Christ, *forgive* is a logical telescoping result of the verb discussed in the previous chapter, *love*. Genuine love results in forgiveness. Those who forgive not, love not. As Sam Calian, president of Pittsburgh Theological Seminary, puts it, "Perhaps we ought to bestow graduates with a masters degree in forgiveness, rather than divinity. This might more accurately describe what our daily objective as Christians ought to be. . . . The essence of Christian faith is forgiveness. Christ is forgiveness in the flesh. Forgiving one another is the human way of loving."[1]

By telling a "parable Jesus didn't tell," one of W. E. Sangster's sermons dramatizes the connection between love and forgive.

> And he arose and set out for his home, and when at last he arrived at the door, he banged and there was no response. He stood there hungry and piteous in his rags, and knocked again and then a third time; finally a window opened and his father looked out and said. "Oh, it's you! You're broke I suppose and you look terrible. Why have you come home? You've had your share of everything. Now I suppose I'll have to feed you!"

And he said: "Father, I have sinned against heaven and in thy sight," but his father banged the window and left him standing on the doorstep. Presently, his father opened the door and said: "You're an utter disgrace to me and to all your relatives. I'm ashamed of you, utterly ashamed. But I'm your father and I've thought it over, and I am prepared to put you on probation for three months, and if, at the end of three months I can find no fault in you, well, perhaps I'll have it in my heart to give you another chance."[2]

Samples from Jesus' Teachings

If your brother sins, rebuke him, and if he repents, forgive him; and if he sins against you seven times in the day, and turns to you seven times, and says, "I repent," you must forgive him. (Luke 17:3-4)

To him who strikes you on the cheek, offer the other also; and from him who takes away your coat do not withhold even your shirt. (Luke 6:29)

[From the cross] Jesus said, "Father, forgive them; for they know not what they do." (Luke 23:34)

[Jesus links our forgiveness of others to God's forgiveness of us] So also my heavenly Father will do to every one of you, if you do not forgive your brother from your heart. (Matthew 18:35; for a fuller picture, see Matthew 18:23-35.)

Judge not, and you will not be judged; condemn not, and you will not be condemned; forgive, and you will be forgiven. (Luke 6:37)

And whenever you stand praying, forgive, if you have anything against any one; so that your Father also who is in heaven may forgive you your trespasses. (Mark 11:25-26)

[In teaching his model prayer, Jesus prays,] "And forgive us our debts, As we also have forgiven our debtors." (Matthew 6:12)

Between Us and God

Few people can manufacture much forgiveness "in-house." Rather, forgiveness is a spiritual matter rooted in our relationship with God. Paul is doing more than making a comparison when he tells the Ephesians to "be kind to one another, tenderhearted, forgiving one another, as God in Christ forgave you" (Eph. 4:32). He means that those who have God in their nature also have forgiveness in their nature.

A little girl in the Philippines reportedly told her priest that she had seen Jesus. She spoke so convincingly that the priest took her to his bishop. The bishop, also impressed, got her an audience with the archbishop. A series of probing questions led to his asking her what Jesus looked like. She described him in vivid detail. Cornered, the archbishop devised a test. "The next time you see him, would you ask him a question for me?" She agreed, and the archbishop said, "Ask him to tell you the last sin the archbishop confessed."

Several weeks later, the little girl phoned to say excitedly that she had just seen Jesus again. The archbishop asked, "Well, did you ask him the question I gave you?"

"Yes," she said.

"Well, what did he tell you?"

"He put his fingers up beside his head like he was confused. Then he said, 'You know, honey, I just can't remember!' "

Jesus says that our forgiveness of others can either block or facilitate the spiritual healing that comes to us from our connection with God. "For if you forgive men their trespasses, your heavenly Father also will forgive you; but if you do not forgive men their trespasses, neither will your Father forgive your trespasses" (Matt. 6:14-15). In his book *The Great Hunger*, a Scandinavian novelist tells of a farmer who loved his beautiful little daughter. One afternoon as the child played in the yard, a neighbor's dog attacked and killed her. The father's bitterness toward the neighbor shook his faith to the core. Shortly after this tragedy, a famine came to that part of the country. The neighbor, who was very poor, had no seed to sow on his land. One night, the distraught father rose from his sleepless bed, dressed in his work clothes, and sowed grain in his neighbor's field. When asked why, he replied, "So that God might live." That was his way of saying what Jesus said, that without love and forgiveness, God cannot live in our lives. Christians at war with their brothers and sisters find it hard to feel peace with their Father.

This is why Jesus says that if you go to church and remember that someone has something against you, you should go and straighten it out and then come back to the altar (see Matt. 5:21-26). If you don't, your cast-iron shield of unforgiveness will barricade you from God. You cannot feel the spiritual presence of a God who forgives through your own protective coating of unforgiveness.

Between Us and Ourselves

In addition to being a spiritual matter between us and God, forgiveness is a psychological matter between us and ourselves. Its presence or absence has enormous internal consequences. As St. Augustine is reported to have said, "If you are suffering from a bad man's injustice, forgive him lest there be two bad men." As George Jean Nathan said, "No man can think clearly when his fists are clenched."

A rape victim was shot in the head by her attacker and left for dead. Although she survived, she was blinded and would wear facial multilations the rest of her life. A television talk show interviewer asked her whether she harbored a lot of resentment and hatred toward the man who did that to her. "No," she said. "I gave that man one night of my life, and I'm not going to give him a second more."

A woman phoned a radio talk show on the subject of loneliness and other problems related to divorce. "Don't forget to forgive," she said. "If you forgive, you can get on with life." Each of these people understood that forgiveness repairs the broken bridges between us and our best selves.

Between Us and Others

In addition to being a spiritual matter between us and God and a psychological matter between us and ourselves, forgiveness is a social matter between us and others. As an icebreaker to let group members introduce themselves, a group leader asked people to tell their names and one thing for which they were thankful. The usual thoughts came out, until one woman said, "My name is Jane, and I'm thankful for erasers." When someone asked why, she said, "Because erasers rub out mistakes." Forgiveness is the emotional eraser that rubs out the mistakes we make with other people and that other people make with us.

Two famous writers of the last century, William Thackeray and Charles Dickens, had great admiration for each other. But one day, as friends sometimes do, they had a heated argument and parted with angry words. When they next met on the street, they pretended not to see each other. A few days after that encounter, they rounded a corner and came face to face. Glaring at each other, they marched on. But Thackeray suddenly turned around and rushed back to Dickens. Grabbing his hand, Thackeray told him he could not bear to keep up this bitterness. Dickens, deeply moved, embraced him, and the two were friends again. It happened just in time; a few days later, Thackeray died.

Regardless of who is right in a personal conflict, nobody really wins. The courage we need to break the ice of frozen social conflict is, however, needed more than it is found. The older we get, the more we seem to lose that kind of courage. A father was in the living room when his daughter came home crying. "I'll never play with her again," she said, speaking of the little girl across the street. "She doesn't like me, and I don't like her!" The father surprised himself and refrained from giving her the scolding advice that came into his mind. About two hours later, the daughter and her neighbor were playing as if nothing had happened. They had patched up their differences. Reflecting on this incident later, the father said to a friend. "Sometimes, I wish I could become as mature as my daughter. As I get older, I forget too many things I ought to remember and remember too many things I ought to forget." He is not alone in this experience.

Refining Our Gold

Forgiveness is the purest form of love. But, like the purest of gold, forgiveness requires the greatest character refinement. If we intend to exhibit God's kind of forgiveness, several questions are in order. The following four are particularly important to that purification process.

Do we forgive criticism? During the late 1960s, six-year-old Ruby Bridges was one of the first black children to integrate the Louisiana school systems. Every day for several weeks, federal marshals picked up Ruby and walked her to school through crowds that screamed, threatened, and cursed her. During this difficult daily walk, Ruby often appeared to be talking to the hecklers. When a reporter asked her about this, she said, "I wasn't talking to them. I was praying for them. They need praying for. That's what God would want me to do."

Criticism is among the hardest hurts to forgive, perhaps because the criticizers do not ask for forgiveness. Yet, God can give us the grace to do it, providing we stay closely connected to him. Henry Bosch reports the conversation between a young pastor and his guide as they began the tour of a coal mine. Near the entrance a beautiful white flower contrasted sharply with its grimy environment. "How can it stay that white?" the pastor asked.

"Throw some coal dust on it and you will see," the guide replied. The young man was amazed to see the fine, black particles slide off the snowy petals. The grime could not adhere to the flower's slick surface.[3] We cannot avoid living in a world of criticism. In spite of our best efforts, people will misunderstand our motives and lash out at us. We will respond in one of two ways: with bitterness or with forgiveness. But the only way we can forgive is by having a strong connection with God in prayer. The power to forgive cannot be manufactured without help from God.

Do we forgive in spite of our feelings? Richard W. DeHaan tells the story of a little boy who had a fight with his brother. The day passed, and the boy continued an unwillingness to speak to his brother. At bedtime, their mother said, "Don't you think you should forgive your brother before you go to sleep? The Bible says we should not let the sun go down on our wrath."

After some perplexed reflection, the boy replied, "But how can I keep the sun from going down?"[4]

Jesus does not condemn anger as a feeling, but he does condemn nurturing the feeling, hanging on to it through our rear-view mirror memory system. When that happens, anger turns to a resentment acid that eats into our soul. In his book *Lee: The Last Years*, Charles Bracelen Flood tells about the time General Robert E. Lee visited a Kentucky home. The woman had lost so much during those terrible years. She took him out to see the remains of a giant old tree in front of the house. Complaining about how it had been mangled by federal artillery fire, she expected Lee to join her in hostility toward the North. But Lee said, "Cut it down, my dear Madam, and forget it."

He was illustrating Jesus' great verb. Forgiveness is not a fussy historian, always preoccupied with who did what to whom. Forgiveness lets the dead past bury the dead past. Forgiveness moves on to the future without needing to settle every outstanding account.

How is that possible? A Christian psychologist gave advice to a woman who had been terribly wronged by her husband and could not find a way to gather up the raveled ends of love and forgiveness. He said, "Prayer is the only answer. Be honest. Say to God, 'I do not feel like loving and forgiving him. I must ask you to love him through me, because I cannot do it by myself.' " Some kinds of forgiveness can happen only in that way. We can loosen our connection with some resentments only by tightening our connection with God.

Do we forgive a lack of perfection? In John Steinbeck's well known story, "The Pearl," a man finds a beautiful pearl. But after close scrutiny he realizes it has one tiny flaw. He takes the pearl to a jeweler, hoping to make it perfect by removing the flaw. His obsession gets the best of him, however. The jeweler peels away layer upon layer of the pearl in an attempt to remove the flaw. Finally, nothing is left. We have no opportunities to develop relationships with perfect people. All of us have flaws. If we cannot accept that, we destroy both the pearl and our own happiness.

In the movie *American Flyer,* a man, in heated anger, tells his older brother: "When someone isn't as strong as you think they should be, did you ever consider forgiving them?" Jesus told a parable about two brothers, in which their father raised a similar question. Like the elder brother in both stories, we always experience a tension between God's call for forgiveness and God's call for proper behavior. Biblical Christianity calls for high moral and ethical standards. How do we treat those who do not hold to these standards, with judgment or tolerance? Biblical Christianity urges people to respond to Christ. How do we treat those who do not respond, with judgment or forgiveness?

This is the old polarity between Law and grace, between high standards and a forgiving spirit. How do we handle that? Only by following the model of Christ—who did both. His teachings repeatedly say, "I have high expectations of you, even higher than the Old Testament Law. But if you fail to meet these expectations, I forgive you and ask you to begin again." The story of the woman being stoned for adultery is one of the numerous instances where he walked through to the other side of this paradox (John 8:3-11). Neither judgment nor forgiveness is enough by itself. Forgiveness without standards leads to chaotic "do as you please" anarchy in personality and behavior. Blanket judgment without forgiveness builds a religious standard impossible for anyone to attain. God treats each of us with a standard we might call "grace in spite of judgment." It is, therefore, incongruous for us to treat others with attitudes and behaviors *less* full of grace than the way God treats us.

Do we make forgiveness an action as well as a thought? In Jane Austen's *Mr. Collins,* one of the characters says, "You ought certainly to forgive them as a Christian, but never to admit them in your sight, or allow their names to be mentioned in your hearing." While this may be the way some "Christians" define forgiveness, it is not a Christian form of forgiveness.

Move the Fence

A pastor tells a story about a company of soldiers during World War II who took the body of their dead comrade to a rural Catholic church in France. They asked if he could be buried in the adjoining cemetery. After asking whether the boy was Catholic and learning that his friends did not know, the priest gave an unpleasant verdict: He must be buried just outside the cemetery fence. The next day, they came back to decorate the grave but could not find it. Then, the priest came out. Following a sleepless night, uneasy with his refusal to allow the burial inside the cemetery, he had risen early and moved the fence so that it now enclosed the soldier's grave. God is forever treating us like that. He reaches out and moves the fence so that we can receive the forgiveness we have not earned, and he asks us to move fences for others.

A small town doctor died after years of dedicated service. His lawyer directed the emptying of his cluttered old office and took the account books to finalize the settlement of the doctor's estate. Flipping through the pages, the lawyer was amazed at the number of times the physician had scribbled the same word across a poor family's charges: *forgiven*.

Christ has written that word across the imperfections in each of our lives. He asks that we learn how to use that word, too.

Discovery Questions for Group Study

1. A strong statement early in this chapter says, "Those who forgive not, love not." Do you agree or disagree? Why?
2. Jesus says in Luke 17:3-4 that we should be willing to forgive people seven times in the same day. Do you think that is always appropriate, or is it sometimes better to withhold forgiveness in order to correct a bad behavior pattern?
3. Do you think it is accurate to say "the stronger our relationship with God, the greater our ability to forgive?"
4. Divide into groups of three or four persons. Ask individuals to share methods they have found helpful in forgiving people who have wronged them.
5. Among the several questions listed in the "Refining Our Gold" section, do you think any stand out as having particular relevance for Christians in your local community? In your congregation? In your denomination?
6. Distribute Bibles and study the passages listed with each *forgive* sample from Jesus' teachings. What point did these words make to people in Jesus' day? What do these words say to you personally? What do these words say to contemporary Christians and contemporary churches?

PART III

How to Help Other People Connect with God

Chapter 7

GO:
SALT
SHAKER
SUGGESTIONS

A young pastor began serving a rural, southern Indiana church. When he put pins in a map to indicate where the members lived, he noticed a strange pattern emerging. The church stood near an intersection where five roads converged. Two of the roads were lined with pins. The other three roads contained only a few. While visiting one of the older church leaders one day, he asked why this was so. "Oh, that's no secret,"she said. "Old Joe Smith used to live up that road. Now he lives down the other road."

We can easily forget that Jesus operated from a three-part, not a two-part, job description. First, he targeted his primary energies on telling and showing people how to connect with God. Second, he described and demonstrated how people who connect with God treat other people. But he did to stop there, set up shop in a local synagogue, and wait for the world to beat a path to those good ideas. His third focus was to tell and to show his followers how to reach out and help other people connect with God. "You are the salt of the earth," he said (Matt. 5:13). "You are the light of the world" (Matt. 5:14). "The harvest is plentiful" (Matt. 9:37). "You shall be my witnesses . . . to the end of the earth" (Acts 1:8). "Go therefore and make disciples" (Matt. 28:19).

Christians in every century act like Joe Smith. Their God connection generates a love for other people that drives them beyond a self-centered spirituality. They go not because it is a duty but because they want others to experience what they have experienced. As John

Chapter 7
Chapter 7

Chapter 7

Wesley put it, "I have one point in view—to promote, so far as I am able, vital practical religion; and by the grace of God to beget, preserve and increase the life of God in the souls of men" (*Letter to Samuel Walker,* 1754).

Samples from Jesus' Teachings

Follow me and I will make you become fishers of men. (Mark 1:17; see also Matthew 4:19; Luke 5:10)

Go into all the world and preach the gospel to the whole creation. (Mark 16:15)

Go and proclaim the kingdom of God. (Luke 9:60; for a fuller picture, see Luke 9:57-62)

Go therefore and make disciples of all nations. (Matthew 28:19; for a fuller picture, see Matthew 28:16-20)

As the Father has sent me, even so I send you. (John 20:21; Jesus said the same thing in his prayer the night before the cross in John 17:18.)

You shall be my witnesses in Jerusalem and in all Judea and Samaria and to the end of the earth. (Acts 1:8)

Other examples and illustrations of this verb appear in Luke 7:22; 14:23; 10:1-20; 15:1-32; 24:44-49.

Related Verbs Jesus Used

Jesus did not say the salt business was simple or easy, but just the opposite. No other verb he used has so many danger signs tacked up around it.

Beware and take heed! "Beware of men; for they will deliver you up to councils, and flog you in their synagogues, and you will be dragged before governors and kings for my sake, to bear testimony before them and the Gentiles" (Matt. 10:17-18). See also Mark 13:9-13.

Shake off the dust! "And wherever they do not receive you, when you leave that town shake off the dust from your feet as a testimony against them" (Luke 9:5).

Flee! "When they persecute you in one town, flee to the next" (Matt 10:23).

Deny! "If any man would come after me, let him deny himself and take up his cross and follow me" (Matt. 16:24). For a fuller picture see Matthew 16:24-27. See also Mark 8:34 and Luke 9:23-26; 14:25-35; 18:22, 28-30.

Do not *despise* one of these little ones. "See that you do not despise one of these little ones . . . it is not the will of my Father who is in heaven that one of these little ones should perish" (Matt. 18:10, 14). See also Matthew 19:13-14, Mark 10:13-14, and Luke 9:48; 18:15-17.

Beware of Substitutes

Jesus frequently used the warning verb *beware* in connection with his instructions to go. How those "bewares" apply vary greatly between the different cultures and centuries in which Christians have lived. The following list reviews some of the most obvious "bewares" of our contemporary English-speaking churches.

Beware of substituting a connection with something else for a connection with Christ. If the season goes sour for a football team, the coach often says, "We need to get back to the basics!" When a business goes downhill, consultants encourage managers to ask themselves the question, "What business are we in here?" Jesus put it this way: "Beware of the leaven of the Pharisees and Sadducees" (Matt. 16:6). He was saying that not everything you can put into bread dough makes it rise. Yeast can get old and lose its potency. Church people of every age tend toward substituting the wrapping paper for the gift, religious rituals for a revolutionizing relationship. If contemporary mainline denominations have made evangelism their "great omission," it is not because they have neglected the priority of evangelism; it is because they have neglected their Christ connection. Jesus says to each of us, "Come to me" (Matt. 11:28). Then he says, "Go into all the world"(Mark 16:15). If we do not come, we cannot effectively go.

Beware of substituting other worthy church goals for the church's primary goal of helping people find God. The title of a song by Jimmy Buffet is "If the Phone Doesn't Ring, It's Me." That would make an appropriate motto for some churches. They have substituted something else for their central task of reaching out to people beyond their walls. Driving through Schaumburg, Illinois, a suburb west of Chicago, a visiting pastor was on his way to church on Palm Sunday. While watching carefully for the church he was seeking, he passed a building that had a large commercial sign that read "Service Center." Next door was another building whose sign read "Recruiting Center" and listed all the armed forces under those two words. Shortly, he passed another sign that read, "Memorial Gardens." These three closely-sequenced signs gave him a new insight. Churches tend to come in three types. Some are memorial gardens; they concentrate on the past, memorializing the coming and going of Jesus Christ to and from the earth. Some churches are service centers; social service to the community is their primary aim. Some churches are recruiting centers; they concentrate on helping people find God. Churches need to accomplish all three functions—helping people remember Christ, helping people serve other people, and helping people connect with God. But recruiting is their basic function. Without that, the other two cannot happen.

A Pennsylvania denominational executive, tells of his family's stay in a dilapidated hotel one summer while on vacation. They had made reservations long in advance, sight unseen. Upon awaking the next morning, they heard the steady thud of a wrecking ball working very close to them. The thuds kept getting closer and closer. Suddenly, they realized that the huge wrecking ball was hitting the very building in which they were housed. They went out into the hall and looked out the window. The hotel was being torn down. Numerical membership declines of the past twenty years are giving many denominational leaders that same horrified feeling. They should not be surprised. History books tell us that always happens to churches that substitute some other worthy goal for Jesus' verb *go*. They are demolished and replaced with those that do.

One of Jesus' warnings to the Pharisees still fits well in our day: "You have a fine way of rejecting the commandment of God, in order to keep your tradition!" (Mark 7:9). Some contemporary denominations reject the "go" of Jesus in order to focus on their ecumenical unity traditions. Other denominations reject the "go" of Jesus in order to focus on a self-satisfied bronzing of their pet biblical interpretation traditions. Still others reject the "go" of Jesus by focusing on the social action traditions developed in the 1960s. All these good things are valid and needed ministries; yet, if substituted for the verb *go*, they become built-in self-destruct mechanisms. Unless people find God, they cannot find God's good causes.

Beware of substituting apathy for caring. A television commercial gives an insightful definition of friendship when it says. "Friends don't let friends drive drunk." One might just as appropriately ask whether a real friend will stand silently by when friends drive their lives without Jesus Christ. Is not driving your life without Jesus Christ approximately equal to driving your automobile without all your faculties intact? Have not friends who are willing to let that happen substituted apathy for caring, often under the guise of not wanting to appear pushy?

While on furlough from missionary service in Africa, Robert Moffat spoke about his work to several audiences in England. A young medical student was in one of those groups. He had hoped to go to the mission field in China, but that country was now closed. He listened in rapt attention as Moffat said, "There is a vast plain to the north, where I have sometimes seen in the morning sun the smoke of a thousand villages where no missionary has ever been." Afterward, the young man said to Moffat, "Would I do for Africa?" That student was David Livingstone, whose explorations opened Africa to the modern era. Today, Moffat's observations would aptly describe thousands of suburban subdivisions. In this century, Jesus' injunction to go applies as much to our cities as to the foreign mission field. When he calls us to care, he is often calling us to care about the people next door.

Beware of substituting thinking for action. A successful salesman said that he always kept his hat on while doing his desk work at the office. When someone asked why, he replied, "That's to remind me that I really ought to be out there instead of in here." A speaker once said in one of his popular motivational lectures that a professor once gave him a definition of character. Character, according to that professor, is the ability to care about a good resolution long after the mood has passed in which you made the decision to do it. Talking about helping people find God is easy, and sometimes it is even mentally stimulating. But talking and thinking can just as easily become substitutes for doing. How often our high moment of inspiration gets dimmed to a one-watt output when the perspiration begins to break out.

An adage from the ancient East is: "It is difficult to satisfy one's appetite by painting pictures of cakes." In evangelism, as in all else, we must take action. Unless our thinking gear shifts into a going gear, other people cannot hear, respond, and become Christians.

Beware of substituting relaxation for commitment. When asked about his denominational preference, comedian Flip Wilson said, "I'm a Jehovah's spectator! I would be a witness, but that would require too much commitment!" A missionary, home to recuperate from her labors, was shopping for a globe of the world to take back to her mission station. The clerk showed her a reasonably priced globe, then another one with a light bulb inside. "This is nicer," the clerk said. "Of course, a lighted world costs more." Christians know that is true, but they are willing to pay the price for a lighted world.

Beware of substituting impersonal methods for personal methods. When Norris Dam, the first Tennessee Valley Authority dam, was built in Appalachia, a worker on the night shift noticed how strange it was to hear the great dynamos humming in the quiet of the night and then look across the lake and see cabins lit with kerosene lamps. When someone asked why this was, he responded that the transmission lines had not been laid yet. More people would light their lives with Christ if Christians would lay effective transmission lines.

In this mass media age, Christians are increasingly tempted to think that mass media—TV, radio, direct mail—are the way to "go." But studies in every denomination indicate that more than three-quarters of all church members first attended the congregations they eventually joined because of one word: *invite.* A regular attender of that congregation said something like, "I would like to invite you to visit our church." So they visited and eventually joined it. When Jesus says "go," he means for us to give our gifts to help people connect with God. One of our most influential gifts is the willingness to invite.

Another effective go strategy comes wrapped in the small and much misunderstood word *witness.* This courtroom term may have confused us, but if we take it literally, we may understand it better. Jesus does not ask us to become lawyers, presenting detailed arguments of the need to believe in God. He asks us to become witnesses. That means telling what we know. A Springfield, Missouri, pastor says,

> Many, feeling they have no special gift for arguments, sit in idleness, when all God wants is their testimony, to tell all they know about him.
>
> In the courtroom, even a small child or an ignorant person can sway both judge and jury by simply relating the facts of the case.
>
> And that is what sways [persons] to Christ, not skillful eloquence, but giving the facts, witnessing to what God has done for us personally, how our lives have been changed by him.[1]

A witness is someone who makes something believable, who closes the credibility gap on the unbelievable. The words of the witness make it possible for the other person to find faith. Jesus was a faithful witness for God. He closed the credibility gap, and he asks us to do that for others. Yet, we often fail to recognize the enormous power in giving or withholding that witness. Al and Lorraine Broom tell of a Seattle businessman who had unknowingly discouraged a business associate from connecting with Christ. Now, the businessman was a long-time Christian, but he had never discussed it with his friend. One day, the friend reported his commitment to Christ at a Billy Graham meeting the night before. The long-time Christian was elated, but the new Christian said, "Friend, you're the reason I have resisted becoming a Christian for all these years. I figured that if a person could live a good life as you do and not be a Christian, there was no need to become one!"[2]

Seeds for the Future

A pastor tells the story of an old man in east Tennessee who thirty years ago had an unusual morning ritual. He would fill a shoulder sack with acorns and take up a wooden stick with a sharpened spike on the end of it. Then he would set out walking over a large burned out forest area in the mountains. Here and there he stopped, poked a hole in the ground, dropped in an acorn, and kicked dirt over it with his boot. When a friend asked him why he did this every day, he said,

"Someone has to think of the future." Today, there is a forest where that man walked. The Christian faith is always one generation away from extinction. Someone has to think about the future. Someone has to think about the people who have not yet connected with Christ. Jesus said that all of us should.

Discovery Questions for Group Study

1. Does a lack of eagerness to invite people to church indicate a lack of strength in your relationship with Christ?
2. In the "Related Verbs Jesus Used" section of this chapter, we find several scriptural instructions for how to behave when people reject our efforts to help them relate to God. Distribute Bibles and study these passages. How do these texts apply to us today?
3. Among the several questions listed in the "Beware of Substitutes" section, do you think any stand out as having particular relevance for Christians in your local community? In your congregation? In your denomination?
4. Distribute Bibles and study the passages listed with each *go* sample from Jesus' teaching. What point did these words make to people in Jesus'day? What do these words say to you personally? What do these words say to contemporary Christians and contemporary churches?

Chapter 8

BAPTIZE: GOD'S WEDDING RING

Two young people stand together at the front of a church. She is dressed in white, he in black. The gold bands, slipped on trembling fingers in the candlelight, do not work instant magic. They do not transform a dating relationship into a mature marital relationship; that takes years and troubles and tears and much trying. But these rings have far more meaning than the commercial value of the metal from which they are made. They signify a new beginning, two people starting in a new direction with new aspirations, new motivations, and new hopes.

As the curtain was falling on the sixth century A.D., a Christian missionary named Augustine landed in Kent, England, with forty missionary teachers. On Christmas Day in 597, Augustine and his helpers baptized ten thousand converts, including the King. Did this water ritual magically transform these pagan people into saintly followers of Jesus? No, but it did signify a new beginning: their determination to start in a new direction with new aspirations, new motivations, and new hopes.

In the summer of 1949, a thirteen-year-old boy was baptized in the waters of Lake Decatur in Central Illinois. Did that exciting and somewhat frightening experience instantly transform him into what Christ had in mind? No, but it was a major life hinge. It signified a new start in a new direction, with new aspirations and new motivations.

In recent years, it has become faddish to question and to discard traditional institutions and rites of passage between life stages. Yet, deep within most of us burns a yearning for the drawing of boundary lines between old and new, between what was and what is to be. Even Thomas J. J. Altizer, a promoter of the short-lived "God Is Dead" theology of the 1960s, had his baby baptized when he thought the child was in danger of dying. Powerful forces in his psyche and Episcopalian background propelled him toward this ancient water ritual—certainly not because he thought it magical, certainly not because he saw it as a scientific, rational way to meet this crisis. Why, then? Because it was sacramental, a religious act considered sacred because it signifies a covenant with divine reality. Like the wedding ring, baptism draws a mark on the ground between past and future. Like the wedding ring, it says, "From this day forward, I stand with God."

Samples from Jesus' Teachings

Go therefore and make disciples of all nations, baptizing them in the name of the Father and of the Son and of the Holy Spirit. (Matthew 28:19)

Truly, truly, I say to you, unless one is born of water and the Spirit, he cannot enter the kingdom of God. That which is born of the flesh is flesh, and that which is born of the Spirit is spirit. (John 3:5-6)

He who believes and is baptized will be saved; but he who does not believe will be condemned. (Mark 16:16)

Then Jesus came from Galilee to the Jordan to John, to be baptized by him. (Matthew 3:13)

And when Jesus was baptized, he went up immediately from the water, and behold, the heavens were opened and he saw the Spirit of God descending like a dove, and alighting on him; and lo, a voice from heaven, saying, "This is my beloved Son, with whom I am well pleased." (Matthew 3:16-17)

Related Words Jesus Used

Unlike most of Jesus' other verbs, *baptize* has no synonym with an identical or similar meaning. It is often, however, closely associated with the verb *repent*. Like the decision to get married and a wedding ring, these two often appear in close sequence with each other.

The word of God came to John the son of Zechariah in the wilderness; and he went into all the region about the Jordan, preaching a baptism of repentance for the forgiveness of sins. (Luke 3:2-3)

> Now after John was arrested, Jesus came into Galilee, preaching the gospel of God, and saying, "The time is fulfilled, and the kingdom of God is at hand; repent, and believe in the gospel." (Mark 1:14)

> Now when the Lord knew that the Pharisees had heard that Jesus was making and baptizing more disciples than John (although Jesus himself did not baptize, but only his disciples), he left Judea and departed again to Galilee. (John 4:1)

Why Be Baptized?

Christian baptism is more frequently practiced than it is understood. Many people who attend church only for Easter, Christmas, weddings, funerals, and ice cream suppers arrange to have their children baptized soon after birth. Many members of denominations that frown on infant baptism act out a similar behavior by their involvement in a baby "dedication" service.

In some European countries where only 3 percent of the population attends worship, 99 percent have been baptized. Other people appear to apply the same perspective to what their denomination calls adult, or believer's, baptism. According to their view, after baptism your eternal fate is sealed. Your cosmic plane ticket is stamped. Regardless of what you do after that day—lie, steal, cheat, gossip, break all the ten commandments the same week—the mortgage on your heavenly mansion is paid off. "Once in grace, always in grace," some of them say. If you are baptized, you are home free. Analysis by an objective sociological observer would probably place these beliefs and actions in a category other than Christian. They seem far more like African witchcraft, Native American rain dances, and common superstition. They seem to view baptism as a magical rite rather than a sacramental action, a superstitious ritual rather than a New Testament concept.

If we discard these less than rational reasons for baptism, what remains? Why should Christians want to be baptized? Why should churches encourage baptism at the beginning point in a God connection? First, because Jesus was baptized (Mark 1:9). If baptism was an important experience for Jesus, how can his followers treat it as a nonessential? Second, because Jesus told us to baptize (Matt. 28:19). Christians have called these instructions the Great Commission. While *baptize* is not the only thing Jesus instructed us to do, its appearance on this list makes it important. Third, because the earliest churches and their successors during the subsequent twenty centuries have baptized. Peter said in his Jerusalem sermon on Pentecost, "Repent, and be baptized every one of you in the name of Jesus Christ" (Acts 2:38). Three thousand people accepted his invitation (Acts 2:41). Paul's letters to the developing churches illustrate that baptism continued to be important (Acts 22:16; Rom. 6:3, 4; I Cor. 12:13; Gal. 3:27; Eph. 4:5; Col. 2:12).

Churches through the centuries have disagreed on the "form" of baptism. Some say total immersion is the only way. Others claim that pouring water on the head is appropriate. Still others have said that a few drops on the forehead is enough. Only an infinitesimal few have practiced what we might call"dry cleaning" baptism, insisting that we are not baptized by water but by the Spirit. However, virtually all churches in all centuries have viewed this rite with the utmost seriousness.

What Does Baptism Mean?

Christians have written tons of words in answer to that question, many of which disagree. Some of these varied interpretations arise because people bring differing viewpoints to baptism. However, much of the disagreement comes from looking at only one part of the New Testament rather than all of the New Testament. Baptism is described in different ways in different scripture verses. We cannot, therefore, summarize its meaning in one sentence.

Baptism is a public declaration of the determination to faithfully follow Jesus Christ. The marriage vows are public statements of personal commitment. In baptism, the Christian is affirming his or her commitment to and faith in Jesus Christ as Lord and Savior. This is the primary reason that some denominations refuse to baptize infants. They feel that baptism is a declaration of personal faith. Since babies cannot make that declaration and parents cannot make it on their behalf, people who hold this belief prefer to wait until baptism becomes a personal choice.

While visiting in Leningrad, a woman heard the story of the 900,000 people who perished in the long siege of Leningrad during World War II. At one point they were trying to save the children—

from both the Nazis and starvation—so they placed them on trucks to cross a frozen lake to safer locations. Many of the mothers, sure that they would never see their children again, yelled to them as they got on the trucks, "Remember your name. Remember your name." Baptism places our name in God's family tree. By our baptism, we commit ourselves to faithfully remember who we are.

Baptism symbolizes repentance of previous ways of life. A story from the early centuries of Christianity tells of a pagan warrior who came to be baptized and to join the Church. The form of baptism used by that congregation was immersion, placing the person completely under the water. The warrior insisted that he did not want his right hand to go under. He wanted to be able to continue doing battle with his enemies. Authentic Christian baptism involves giving up our old ways and putting our sword hands under, too. Peter makes this clear in his sermon on the Church's birth day in Jerusalem: "Repent, and be baptized every one of you" (Acts 2:38).

Baptism symbolizes forgiveness of sins. An elderly woman in a small Midwestern community phoned her banker to find out how to dispose of a large bond she had received as an inheritance. The banker asked, "Is this bond for conversion or redemption?"

After a long pause, she said, "Sonny, am I talking to the First National Bank or the first parish church?" Both of these are descriptions of what happens in baptism—conversion and redemption. In the same sentence where Peter urges repentance, he says we are baptized for the forgiveness of sins" (see Acts 2:38). No matter how wrong we have been or how badly we have behaved, God wipes the chalkboard clean with the water of baptism.

Baptism symbolizes entry into a new life with Christ. The young pastor in a student church was preparing to conduct his first baptismal service. The old church had a baptismal tank set in the floor with a wooden lid over it. Since he realized that the lack of modern water heating equipment would make getting the water ready an arduous undertaking, the pastor asked a lay leader, "Who usually handles this?"

"I always take care of it," the man said. "Don't worry about a thing." The layman was the funeral director for the community, a very dependable individual, so the pastor was happy to trust the matter to his capable hands.

When he arrived for the service, the pastor found the tank ready, the water just the right temperature. But spread on the floor all around the tank were the green mats used around graves in the cemetery. On either side stood banks of flowers like those usually found beside caskets. The young pastor was shocked, but then realized that the symbolism was thoroughly biblical. Paul said very clearly that baptism is a symbol of death to the old self in order that a new self may be born in Christ. "We were buried therefore with him by baptism into death, so that as Christ was raised from the dead by the glory of the Father, we too might walk in newness of life" (Rom. 6:4; see also Gal. 3:27 and Col. 2:12; 3:1-11).

Baptism symbolizes entrance into church membership. None of us can choose the biological family into which we will be born. In baptism, we can make a choice. By being baptized, we are saying that we want to be born into the family of God, that we want to wear the family name (Christian), that we want to live in the family home (the church), that we want to sit at the family table (the Lord's table). Baptism is a personal matter, but it is not a private matter. Baptism always involves three participants: God, the body of Christ (the Church), and the individual. Notice what happened after Peter's Jerusalem sermon: "So those who received his word were baptized, and there were added that day about three thousand souls. And they devoted themselves to the apostles' teaching and fellowship, to the breaking of bread and the prayers" (Acts 2:41-42). See Acts 9:18-19 and 16:15-40 for other evidence that baptism was viewed as a rite of admission to the Church.

The New Testament record does not indicate that people were baptized into specific local congregations. Rather, their baptism was a symbol of admission to the Church universal. Paul writes, "For by one Spirit we were all baptized into one body—Jews or Greeks, slaves or free—and all were made to drink of one Spirit" (I Cor. 12:13). Paul was baptized only once. He was not baptized again as he moved from church to church across Asia Minor. Barnabas was baptized only once. Timothy was baptized only once.

Baptism symbolizes entry into eternal life. As part of his long discourse on baptism, Paul says, "But if we have died with Christ, we believe that we shall also live with him. For we know that Christ being raised from the dead will never die again; death no longer has dominion over him" (Rom. 6:8-9). This does not mean that eternal life comes by the act of baptism. To say that we are saved by our baptism would be logic as faulty as that the Pharisees used in thinking they were saved by their burnt offerings. We are not saved by an action. Baptism no more guarantees salvation than a good wedding ceremony guarantees a good marriage. We are saved through our continuing faith-filled relationship with Jesus Christ. He, and he alone, is the source of salvation.

Baptism symbolizes a starting line. When Jesus was baptized, he left his carpenter shop in Galilee and took up his ministry to the world. Receiving the Spirit of God at baptism meant a new life, a new work, a new beginning, and our baptism is the same. Baptism is not a culmination of our faith, a sign that we are safely across the finish line. Rather, it says that we are starting the race; we are beginning the Christian life. We are saying with this public action of our physical bodies that we are committing both body and spirit to a new beginning in relationship with Christ. We will want to take many other actions as part of this relationship—praying, studying, working in the church, serving —so that we may "grow in the grace and knowledge of our Lord and Savior Jesus Christ" (II Pet. 3:18) and move closer to achieving a "measure of the stature of the fulness of Christ" (Eph. 4:13). But baptism marks the beginning point.

More Than Water

A light bulb has no value when it is separated from electric current. By itself, it is not light. It is an instrument of the light. It bears witness to the light. If all we get when we are baptized is the water, we only get wet. Baptism is the instrument of something beyond itself—the redeeming, transforming light that was in Christ and is now in us.

Roger Russ of New Zealand says that we can understand baptism better if we drop our arguments about the proper age of candidates, the right amount of water, and the appropriate type of service. He suggests that we view this matter from a larger perspective by remembering that the word *baptism* came into the English language from a Greek word meaning to "dip under, plunge, or immerse." He notes that we often speak of people being immersed in their work, sports, or politics.

There is more to baptism than being immersed in water. We are so immersed in Christ that some of his qualities and priorities begin to be seen in us. Some Christians—the Quakers, for example—have not been baptized by any amount or mode of water baptism, either as infants or adults. Yet, those persons are clearly immersed in Christ. The light from their close relationship with him gleams through the love in their lives. Russ says, therefore, that

> The reality or otherwise of our baptism depends on whether or not we are immersed in Christ rather than whether or not we have been immersed in water.
>
> The purpose of the service (sacrament) of Christian baptism is to celebrate, to symbolise and to put the seal, on our relationship with Christ. It positively and meaningfully affirms that relationship, but it does not create it.
>
> The debate on such questions, as to whether or not baptism should be administered by sprinkling, pouring, or immersion and whether it should be . . . reserved for those who are mature enough to profess their own faith should be seen for what it is. In the long run it is not a debate about what christian baptism is. It is a debate about the appropriate way to celebrate and seal the baptism into Christ of those whom he has already claimed to be his and about the appropriate stage of their growth in faith and commitment to him for such a significant celebration to take place.
>
> Recognizing that the "one baptism" of the New Testament consists in the fact that we are immersed in Christ rather than that we have been immersed in water frees us to accept the reality of the baptism of those whose baptismal practices differs markedly from our own. And it opens the way for us to accept one another as members of the one church of our Lord Jesus Christ.[1]

More Than a Ring

Baptism is not a magical act, though it often marks a mysterious transformation in personality. Neither is baptism a purely symbolic act, though it does point beyond itself to a transcendent reality, which human logic cannot fully understand and science cannot fully measure. Baptism is a mystical act that witnesses a transaction, not just with water, but with Spirit. A wedding ring is much more than a golden band placed on the left hand's ring finger, and baptism is much more than the touch of water in a special way. Like the ring, it is the outward expression of an inward experience.

In Jesus' story of the prodigal son (Luke 15:11-32), when the wayward boy returned home after his failures in the far country, his father ran out to meet him and kissed him. The Father ordered the servants to give the boy a ring, a robe, and shoes. There was nothing magical about that ring of welcome, but it was full of deep significance. It symbolized the father's love. It symbolized the father's forgiveness. It symbolized a family reunion. It symbolized the chance for a new life. Why be baptized? It symbolizes the Father's love and forgiveness, entering the Father's house, and beginning the new life that relationship brings.

Discovery Questions for Group Study

1. This chapter makes a strong comparison between establishing a marriage relationship through the wedding ceremony and establishing a relationship with God through baptism. With a marriage, divorce dissolves the relationship. Are there ways by which people can dissolve their baptism relationship?

2. Divide into two groups. Ask one group to list every possible reason why baptizing infants is a good idea. Ask the other group to list every possible reason why it is a good idea to baptize people only after they reach an age at which they can personally state their beliefs in Christ. Ask a reporter from each group to present these reasons to the entire group. Discuss any new insights that may emerge from this process.

3. Ask one of the group members to obtain material from your pastor in order to make a brief presentation regarding your denomination's traditional interpretation of baptism. Discuss.

4. The "What Does Baptism Mean?" section reviews seven different meanings for baptism. To which of these do you think greatest emphasis is given in your denomination? Least emphasis?

5. If baptism is "Spirit rather than water" and "relationship rather than ritual," why bother to use the water and the ritual at all?

6. Distribute Bibles and study the passages listed with each "baptize" sample from Jesus' teachings. What point did these words make to people in Jesus' day? What do these words say to you personally? What do these words say to contemporary Christians and contemporary churches?

Chapter 9

TEACH: LAMPLIGHTER POWER

Scottish singer Harry Lauder once told the story of a lamplighter who passed his house each night. As the old man zigzagged his way down the street, lighting the various gas lamps, Lauder soon lost sight of him. But he knew where the lamplighter was by the avenue of light he left behind him.

Down through the centuries, Jesus and his followers lit a similar trail of light. Historian Herbert Butterfield says,

> The ordinary historian, when he comes, shall we say, to the year 1800 does not think to point out to his readers that in this year, still, as in so many previous years, thousands and thousands of priests and ministers were preaching the Gospel week in and week out, constantly reminding the farmer and the shopkeeper of charity and humility, persuading them to think for a moment about the great issues of life, and inducing them to confess their sins. Yet this was a phenomenon calculated greatly to alter the quality of life and the very texture of human history; and it has been the standing work of the church throughout the ages. Even under the worst of popes, there was a light that never went out.[1]

Teacher was the description most frequently applied to Jesus by his peers. More than thirty times, the Gospel writers record that people called him that. Again and again, we hear phrases like, "And he opened his mouth and taught them, saying" (Matt. 5:2). When he sent the disciples out to expand his effort to help people connect with God, teaching was one of the key strategies in their game plan: "teaching them to observe all that I have commanded you" (Matt. 28:20). Teaching is still the primary way Christianity is transmitted.

"Going" is the critical first step. "Saying" is what happens after we go. Teaching is like the fuel in the lamplighter's stick; it furnishes the light power for our going and saying.

Teaching is not the private preserve of pastors and Sunday school teachers. We all have this power, and we all use it for either good or ill. Someone said that the mother of Henry David Thoreau made it impossible for him to be a Christian and that the mother of John Wesley made it impossible for him to be anything else. Through her teaching, Susannah Wesley gave light to millions in her generation and to billions in coming generations. That awesome power is part of the job description/opportunity package for every Christian. We all teach. By our words and our deeds we all teach and influence other people—not just our children, but everyone around us. By teaching what Jesus told us, we become lamplighters for God, leaving an avenue of light in this generation and the next and the next.

Samples from Jesus' Teachings

[In the argument between Mary and Martha regarding which was the better behavior—taking care of the guests or listening to the Master's teachings—Jesus said his words were more important than the work.] "Martha, Martha, you are anxious and troubled about many things; one thing is needful. Mary has chosen the good portion, which shall not be taken away from her." (Luke 10:41-42)

No one after lighting a lamp puts it in a cellar or under a bushel, but on a stand, that those who enter may see the light. Your eye is the lamp of your body; when your eye is sound, your whole body is full of light; but when it is not sound, your body is full of darkness. Therefore be careful lest the light in you be darkness. If then your whole body is full of light, having no part dark, it will be wholly bright, as when a lamp with its rays gives you light. (Luke 11:33-36)

And when they had finished breakfast, Jesus said to Simon Peter, "Simon, son of John, do you love me more than these?" He said to him, "Yes, Lord; you know that I love you." He said to him, "Feed my lambs." A second time he said to him, "Simon, son of John, do you love me?" A second time he said to him, "Simon, son of John, do you love me?" He said to him,

"Yes, Lord; you know that I love you." He said to him, "Tend my sheep." He said to him the third time, "Simon, son of John, do you love me?" Peter was grieved because he said to him the third time, "Do you love me?" And he said to him, "Lord, you know everything; you know that I love you." Jesus said to him, "Feed my sheep." (John 21:15-17)

All authority in heaven and on earth has been given to me. Go therefore and make disciples of all nations, baptizing them in the name of the Father and of the Son and of the Holy Spirit, teaching them to observe all that I have commanded you; and lo, I am with you always, to the close of the age. (Matthew 28:18-20)

What Should We Teach?

Christian teachers have one basic textbook: the Bible, particularly the New Testament. Teachers through the ages have stressed three additional sources of authority: reason, the traditions of the Church, and insights from the Holy Spirit that are tested by experience. Each of these three must, however, be viewed as a servant to our basic textbook, the Bible. Thus arguments about biblical interpretation quite naturally produce the biggest fights in churches and denominations. Each generation of leaders knows that determining what parts of the textbook will be emphasized most and what those parts mean always determines the future shape of the faith, the Church, and of the Church's ministry.

What, then, should Christians teach? A simple and obvious answer is the biblical basics. But what are the biblical basics? Teachers in various denominations will vary their emphasis due to the influence of reason, their Church's traditions, and their understanding of insights from the Holy Spirit. But a holistic biblical Christianity would surely include the following twenty centering point basics:

1. *God centered*. When Jesus taught about God, he most often described him as a "seeking God who cares," not as a "judgmental God who is eager to burn you in hell if you do not mend your ways" or a "waiting God who sits idly around heaven, wishing his children would come home."

2. *Christ centered*. Christ is our central focus, our "Bible," our way of knowing the nature of God.

3. *Holy Spirit centered*. The Holy Spirit is one of the primary ways God communicates with us.

4. *Bible centered*. Since the Bible is our primary source for knowing the mind of Christ, it is our primary guidebook for living.

5. *Spiritual reality centered*. We take seriously the spiritual side of human life, which Jesus called the kingdom of God. This means we are rational but *more* than rational, emotional but *more* than emotional.

6. *Prayer centered*. Prayer is the primary way we maintain our personal relationship with God.

7. *Reason centered*. The mind is the primary tool for receiving the revelation that comes to us through the Bible and the Holy Spirit.

8. *Repentance centered*. We take sin and evil seriously as a reality in personal human life, not just in the social and political structures of our life together.

9. *Faith centered*. Our continuous relationship with God empowers us to do loving actions toward our neighbors. Remembering Paul's struggle against legalism and Martin Luther's struggle against indulgences, we avoid the temptation to adopt a "works righteousness" theology, which says that what we do as Christians is more important than our relationship with God.

10. *Personal experience centered*. Christian faith cannot be defined as intellectual assent to a list of religious doctrines; it is a trusting relationship with God.

11. *Trust centered*. Confidence in an ever-present God who will meet our needs (faith in his providential care) lifts us above secular psychological and sociological efforts at self-salvation.

12. *Joy centered*. Because of our trusting connection with God, we can rejoice in all things that happen in our lives and circumstances (see Phil. 4:4).

13. *Hope centered*. The future is in God's hands, not ours. This hopefulness encompasses the future both before death and beyond death.

14. *Love centered*. Love is our rule book for relationships with other persons.

15. *Forgiveness centered*. Because God takes sin seriously but forgives us (gives us grace when we do not deserve it), we do the same for others.

16. *Discipleship centered*. One of the primary results of our relationship with God is our increased motivation to accomplish his work in the church and world.

17. *Human need centered*. Meeting human needs is a higher goal than urging people to conform to religious forms and rituals.

18. *Church centered*. Solitary faith is not reported in the New

Testament. Christian faith is a group process, which is ignited and nourished in faith communities.

19. *Tolerance centered.* God calls us and our denomination to a level of perfection in thought, words, and deeds that we do not achieve. Therefore, we tolerate imperfections in other Christians and denominations. This propels us toward a unity orientation regarding other denominations.

20. *Freedom centered.* Tolerance makes freedom of thought our game plan for unity among all Christians.*

The Big Three

Three trees stand far taller than the other twenty. These three produced the seed from which the others grew. Without their protection, the others cannot stand through the storms and continue to grow. The following three questions, therefore, can help keep our teaching close to its original basics:

Do We Teach Jesus? Due to Copernicus, we have learned that earth is not the center of things; the sun is. In every spiritual revolution in history, Christians have rediscovered an eternal truth: Our rational thinking ability is not the center; the Son is. Printers use *italicized letters* in order to create words that appear to lean forward and upward. This unusual forward slant draws attention to something special, such as a book title or the name of a ship. Jesus was God's *italics* in the print of humankind. Without God's Son, the Church could not have sprung to life, and the Bible would be a forgotten Hebrew book. Churches retain their effectiveness only by concentrating on this special Word. Without this special Word, churches have little of significance to say in a society already overloaded with special interest groups trying to attract customers and participants.

One crisp winter evening, a pastor got an astronomy lesson from his teenage son. About forty-five degrees up from the horizon in the northern sky, the boy pointed to the North Star. He pointed out that the other constellations—Taurus, Pegasus, Orion, and all the others—as the night wears on rotate like the hands of a clock around

---

*Adapted from *Moving Toward a Biblical Theology of Evangelism* by Herb Miller. Copyright © 1987 by Net Press. Used by permission.

that fixed constellation. They move during each hour of the night, but it never moves. That is why sailors in every century since they first got free from the coastlines have used the North Star to steer in the right direction. It is always a reliable point of reference. It does raise or lower about twenty-three degrees in reference to the horizon between summer and winter. But while everything else in the heavens shuffles around, it basically stands still. God did that same thing for us when he sent Jesus to a stable in Bethlehem. Jesus is the polar star against which we can measure everything else. His life and teachings stand eternally as God's handwriting across the face of humanity. By him, we can set the compasses of our small lives, regardless of how lost or out of touch they become.

Study the other world religions, and you will find some sparkle and some guidance. But they are to the life of Christ like the drifting constellations of the universe around the North Star. They have some value. They make a contribution. They speak to us of life's deeper meanings. They point toward better ways in our relationship with God and other people. But they cannot substitute for the North Star. "I am the way, and the truth, and the life; no one comes to the Father, but by me" (John 14:6). These others improve the quality of our journey, but this Star illustrates the destination and how to get there.

Do We Teach the Bible? The immense popularity of various types of Bible study among contemporary young adults illustrates the great truth that we have no other reliable way to know the mind of Christ except through the Bible. Alexander Solzhenitsyn, describing one of the striking memories of his imprisonment, told of the man who slept in the bunk above his. In that horrendous situation, the man remained serene, cheerful, and brotherly. Solzhenitsyn began to watch the man carefully. Each evening when the man lay down in his bunk, he pulled out of his pockets small pieces of paper on which words were scribbled. Solzhenitsyn discovered that the scribblings were words copied from the Gospels. Through those words, this prisoner was delivered from brokenness and bitterness and transformed into a loving, encouraging light to others. Countless stories from every century illustrate that same truth. These words have a power above the level of normal printed pages. They can become *the word* to us and to our circumstances; that is what keeps the Gideons distributing their Bibles. Countless people, in the most unusual of ways and places, find the seed of these words coming up through the cracks in their lives and turning them into new people.

A visitor at a World's Fair tells about entering a large denominational church exhibit. It contained a display with all kinds of machine-operated panels and buttons and gadgets. By pressing a single button, you could obtain information on foreign missions, social outreach, and many other items of interest. But as he reached out to press one of the buttons on the panel, the man noticed a small sign that read: "Out of Order." We can survive with many aspects of our church organizations out of order, but if our transmission of the Bible is out of order, we cannot function as authentic Christians.

Do We Teach Prayer? Christ is the mind of God. The Bible is a written record of the mind of God. Prayer opens the door that lets the mind of God into our thinking and behavior. The average person is more highly aware of this than we might imagine. When eighty thousand readers of *Better Homes and Gardens* responded to the survey question "Faced with a spiritual dilemma, what guides you most?" 68 percent of them answered "prayer/meditation."[2]

Paul Robbins, in reporting the death of spiritual giant Harold John Ockenga, lists his accomplishments and the secret to his successes. A pastor for thirty-five years, Ockenga helped launch Billy Graham's ministry. Co-founder of Fuller Theological Seminary, he served as its first president and as the first president of the National Association of Evangelicals. While president of Gordon College, he presided over the merger of Gordon Divinity School and the Conwell Theological Seminary and became the first president of Gordon-Conwell Theological Seminary. Author of fourteen books, he chaired the board of Christianity Today, Inc., for twenty-five years.

Robbins says that he and Harold Myra once asked Ockenga the question: "How did one person get so much done and still maintain physical, emotional, and spiritual health?"

Ockenga replied, "I have always been very busy, but there is a secret. You can do it all right if you keep a prayer list. I've kept one for forty-one years, and everything goes on that list. I write a brief summary of the petition; I number it and date it. When it's answered, I write across it, 'Answered.' "

When they asked him how he found time to pray, he said, "I pray every morning. First I exercise, shave and bathe. Then I pray until breakfast, picking up where I left off on my prayer list. I've had this prayer habit from the time I went to college."[3]

The apostle Paul puts it this way: "No wonder we do not lose heart! Though our outward humanity is in decay, yet day by day we are inwardly renewed" (II Cor. 4:16 NEB). When Christians maintain their prayer connection; they maintain their God connection and God's continuous method of teaching them his mind.

Our Shadow Selves

I have a little shadow that goes in and out with me,
And what can be the use of him is more than I can see.
He is very, very like me from the heels up to the head;
And I can see him jump before me, when I jump into my bed.

That nursery rhyme is an apt description of the influence our teaching has on people around us. Although we are not all professional teachers, we all teach. For good or bad, better or worse, what we teach influences the people around us—often permanently. For the Christian, two questions are particularly important.

Do we teach our children the faith? In our contemporary society, one that highly esteems education, we find a strange silence regarding the need for the spiritual education of children; yet, all the evidence runs the other direction. More than 85 percent of Christians make their initial decision prior to the age of eighteen. When Jesus said, "Let the children come to me" (Matt. 19:14), he was stating a major spiritual principle.

In these days, when democracy is so highly valued, some people conclude that children need to make up their own minds about matters of faith. True, they do; yet, we can easily misunderstand the process by which that happens. A church newsletter gives a perspective on this matter by describing the pastor's visit to a home.

"Come in, pastor," said the mother.

"Beautiful day, isn't it?" said the father.

"Grubblefleediddy!" said the nine-year-old son.

As they sat down, the boy began working a puzzle on the living room floor, moving the pieces very intelligently. But he interrupted the adult conversation several times with statements like "Stibbfinkleybob!" The parents did not seem to notice.

But finally, when the boy brought his pet for the pastor to admire, the two had to attempt a direct conversation. Then, the mother explained: "If you have trouble understanding Junior, it's because we haven't taught him English yet."

"Oh," said the pastor, "why not?"

"Well, there are so many good languages in the world that we didn't want to force ours on him. So we thought we'd wait until he's twenty-one and let him choose which one he wants to speak."

And Junior said, "Schkilippity, vonzerpalleptity!"[4]

2. *Do we teach the faith by our life-style and behavior?* It is said that author and historian Thomas Carlyle once received a letter from someone who said, "Mr. Carlyle, I wish to be a teacher. Will you tell me the secret of successful teaching?" Carlyle reportedly responded with, "Be what you would have your pupils to be. All other teaching is unblessed mockery and apery."

When we carry a full bucket of water and bump into someone, some of the water sloshes out. When we come into contact with other people, what we have inside inevitably sloshes out. Greed or guilt or anger always spills on others. So do love, caring, and happiness. Yes, we all have a little shadow that goes in and out with us—the shadow of what we teach by word and deed. That shadow influences the people around us, either for better or for worse.

Walking Bible

Many years ago, a trial was beginning at the courthouse in a small county seat town. But when officials prepared to swear in the first witness, they could not find the old Bible they had used for years. A quick search of the courthouse revealed nothing. Finally, the judge called the bailiff forward and whispered in his ear. "Go down to the county clerk's office and get Ed," he said.

Ed had been an elder in a local church longer than anyone could remember. He was a shining example of what the Christian faith is all about. In a few minutes, the bailiff approached the bench with Ed in tow. The judge said, "Ed, you have communicated more of the Bible to more people than most of the Bibles in this town. You will make a good substitute for the one we can't find." And so, the first witness placed his hand on Ed's head, swore the oath, and the trial began.

If you want to test your proficiency with Jesus' verb *teach* ask yourself these questions: Would a judge ask me to substitute for a Bible? If not, am I willing to move in that direction by resolving to move my life in new directions?

Discovery Questions for Group Study

1. Is it necessary for us to use words in our teaching, or is the example of our Christian behavior a better way to teach?
2. Ask three or more group members to tell about the person in their lives who most strongly influenced them to come closer to God. As they share those experiences, ask them to indicate the ways by which that person's teaching was communicated in words and the ways by which it was communicated in behavior.
3. In the "What Should We Teach?" section, ask people to check the seven items that they feel are emphasized most in your congregation's teaching at the present time. To get a picture of what your group thinks, read each of the twenty points aloud and ask members of the group to hold up their hands if they checked that particular one. Note the totals on a flip chart.
4. Among the questions in "The Big Three" section, do you think any stand out as having particular relevance for Christians in your local community? In your congregation? In your denomination?
5. Distribute Bibles and study the passages listed with each "teach" sample from Jesus' teachings. What point did these words make to people in Jesus' day? What do these words say to you personally? What do these words say to contemporary Christians and contemporary churches?

Chapter 10

SERVE:
GOD'S PERSONNEL

A little boy who had grown up in a small country church attended
worship with his parents in a large city congregation. As they entered
the front door, he was amazed when an usher pinned a red ribbon on
his lapel. Printed on the ribbon in bright gold letters was the word
visitor. On the way to the local cafeteria for lunch after church, he
tugged at his father's sleeve and asked, "Why don't they give the
members of the church red ribbons, too? How come only the visitors
get them?"

His father replied "If you gave the members ribbons, what would
you print on them so you could tell them apart from the visitors?"

"Personnel," the little boy replied.

That noun captures the meaning of another great verb Jesus
suggested his disciples build into the guidance system of their
lives—*serve*. "Whoever would be great among you must be your
servant . . . even as the Son of man came not to be served but to
serve, and to give his life as a ransom for many" (Matt. 20:26-28).

When Orion N. Hutchinson, Jr., was named editor of church
school publications for The United Methodist Church, he said,

> My hope for the church is that it will learn anew the central
> focus of servanthood. This means we are called to be servants of
> the Word and the world. We are first to lay hold upon the Word
> for our mandate, our marching orders, our spiritual sustenance,
> and our ultimate hope. Then, we are to move out to be servants
> to the world of human need and spiritual ignorance, bringing
> what we have learned as it influences word and deed.[1]

Hutchinson's statement magnificently weaves together three great
biblical truths:

"Serve" is the primary way God accomplishes his will in the world. When God wants to make an improvement, does he set his radio alarm for 5:30 A.M., eat a hearty breakfast, pull on his coveralls, and lace up his work shoes? No, he usually sends some of his personnel to do it. When he wanted the Jews out of Egyptian slavery, he sent a person to do it: Moses. When he wanted them to know the truth about righteousness, justice, and mercy, he sent prophets to tell it: Isaiah, Jeremiah, Ezekiel, Daniel. When he wanted racial equality in America, he sent a person to get it started: Martin Luther King, Jr.

"Serve" is the way Jesus accomplished his mission. Crosses come in over four hundred shapes. Forty of these appear in Christian art. Some of the best known are the Tau (T), Roman (†), Greek (+), and St. Andrew's (X). The cross remains the central symbol of Christianity because it captures in picture form the essence of how Christ accomplished God's objectives.

"Serve" is the way Jesus told his disciples to work. When we speak of someone's making the decision to become a pastor, we often use phrases like "preparing for full-time Christian service." Such descriptions are misleading. Jesus calls all Christians to full-time service. The only question is how we will serve.

Samples from Jesus' Teachings

He who is greatest among you shall be your servant. (Matthew 23:11; for a fuller picture, see Matthew 23:2-11.)

Whoever would be great among you must be your servant, and whoever would be first among you must be your slave; even as the Son of man came not to be served but to serve, and to give his life as a ransom for many. (Matthew 20:26-28; for a fuller picture, see Matthew 20:17-28; see also Mark 10:32-45.)

You are the light of the world. A city set on a hill cannot be hid. Nor do men light a lamp and put it under a bushel, but on a stand, and it gives light to all in the house. Let your light so shine before men, that they may see your good works and give glory to your Father who is in heaven. (Matthew 5:14-16)

If any one would be first, he must be last of all and servant of all. (Mark 9:35)

Salt is good; but if the salt has lost its saltness, how will you season it? Have salt in yourselves. (Mark 9:50; for a fuller picture, see Mark 9:33-50.)

Related Verbs Jesus Used

Since service is the platform on which Jesus lived and called others to live, illustrations of *serve* and other verbs like it appear in almost every New Testament chapter.

I must work the works of him who sent me. (John 9:4)
I must be about my Father's business. (Luke 2:49)
He began to wash the disciples' feet. (John 13:1-17)
Well done, good and faithful servant. (Matthew 25:14-30)
Go, sell what you have, and give to the poor. (Matthew 19:21)
Inasmuch as you have done it to the least of these. (Matthew 25:34-46)
Feed my sheep. (John 21:15-17)
The harvest is great, but the laborers are few. (Luke 10:1)
Do good to your enemies. (Luke 6:35)
Do to others what you want them to do to you. (Matthew 7:12)

Catching Our Own Passes

In football, the passer-receiver transaction normally flows in only one direction. The passer throws; the receiver catches. Life at its best is more like tennis than football; the more we serve, the more we receive. This happens in at least three major ways:

Serving increases our emotional receiving. It is said that Albert Schweitzer once stated, "I don't know what your destiny will be, but one thing I know; the only ones among you who will be really happy are those who have sought and found how to serve." All the data seems to point in that direction. Someone asked ninety-three-year-old Grandma Moses what she was proudest of. "I've helped some people," she replied. After more than thirty years of spending Christmas overseas entertaining members of the armed service, comedian Bob Hope said that he got satisfaction out of that kind of sacrifice. A telephone caller on a radio talk show, whose topic for the day was loneliness, said, "I am a widow, and I find that the best cure for loneliness is to get out and do something for someone else." Life does not offer its best on easy terms. Its best comes through service. We make a living by what we get, but we make a life by what we give.

In connecting with other people through service, we break out of the awful prison of loneliness into which all of us are born the first time. Caring for others is a God-powered artesian energy bubbling up within us. If we cap that well, we begin to die of emotional thirst. That truth is at the core of what Jesus meant when he said, "It is more blessed to give than to receive" (Acts 20:35). His list of beatitudes (Matt. 5:3-11) affirms the same principle. Giving, not getting, brings a state of blessed meaning to our lives.

Serving increases the help we receive from others. One of the great lawmakers of the twentieth century, Carl Hayden, entered office in 1913. After the swearing in ceremony, Congressman Joshua Talbott of Maryland told the young Arizonan that there are two kinds of congressmen, show horses and work horses. Talbott suggested that if Hayden wanted the respect and help of his colleagues he should try to be a work horse. Talbott had learned what Hayden also learned, the principle of serving and receiving.

As preparations were being made for a battle in the Revolutionary War, a corporal arrogantly ordered his men to lift a heavy beam. A man in civilian clothes who was walking by said, "Why don't you help them?"

"Sir,"he replied indignantly, "I am a corporal!"

The man in civilian dress apologized for his misperception, stripped off his coat and helped the soldiers himself. When the job was finished, he said, "Corporal, the next time your men need help, call on your commander-in-chief. I'll be glad to help." With that, George Washington put on his coat and left. Like every truly great leader, he understood the principle of serving and receiving.

Serving increases our probability of success in every undertaking. When the famous preacher Phillips Brooks was asked to name the first thing he would do if called to pastor a poor, dying church, he said he would take up the largest offering he could for missions. He understood the principle of success by serving.

While imprisoned in 1930, Mahatma Gandhi translated the poem, "True Religion," written by sixteenth-century Hindu poet Tulsi Das, from its original Sanskrit. One verse reads:

> Nothing is hard to him, who casting life aside
> Thinks only this
> How may I serve my fellow man?

Gandhi, too, had learned the principle of success by serving.

To Be Specific

Each new generation of Christians must ask a new set of questions in order to keep its serving on track. The following three would surely be among the most important for our present generation.

Is our serving a service to Christ, or is it merely a service to our own self-satisfaction? As we noted earlier in this chapter, serving increases our emotional receiving. And yet, if directed only toward the goal of self-satisfaction, our serving lacks stamina. Without a high commitment to a cause higher than ourselves, we are inclined to go home for a nap when the going gets tough. Sprawled out in gigantic letters across the front of an impressive brick building in Atlanta, Georgia, are the words

> The Salvation Army
> Southern Territory Headquarters
> Serving Others Through Christ

Whoever designed that sign understood and stated an easily forgotten principle. Our main power source is outside ourselves. Few people long persist in tough kinds of service if motivated only by self-satisfaction.

Is our serving action oriented or merely public image oriented? Someone asked a West Texas farmer how his wheat crop was looking. "Pretty good," he said with a farmer's characteristic understatement, then added an explanation. "When our wheat was putting on heads, we got some good rains. The stalks were short and thin, but the heads were big and full. We got ours planted early, and I guess that helped. A lot of the wheat in the county was not yet at the head stage when the rains came. So, the stalks grew tall and thick, but the heads are small, the grains in them are scrawny, and the yield will be low."

Farmers are in the wheat business, not the wheat stalk business. They cannot take a wheat field to the bank; they can take only the wheat. Because we wish others to think well of us, we are prone to substitute image for action. But fruit is the objective of Christian service, not recognition or the holding of church offices. "You will know them by their fruits," Jesus said (Matt. 7:20). The ultimate aim of Christian life is not to look good but to do good. God calls us to serve, not just to shine.

Is our serving and giving sufficient to counterbalance our natural tendency toward selfishness and getting? A survey indicates that 71 percent of college freshmen say they are getting a higher education in order to be able to make more money.[2] This is up considerably since the 1960s. Yet, the percentage of Americans who volunteer to help with charitable activities—such as working with the underprivileged, the infirm, or the elderly—has soared in recent years. Among adult citizens of the United States, 39 percent do volunteer work, compared with 27 percent in 1977.[3] How do we explain these two opposite trends? By the permeation of Christian teaching in society and by instinct, people know that Jesus was right when he said, "Take heed, and beware of all covetousness; for a man's life does not consist in the abundance of his possessions" (Luke 12:15). They know that life, in order to have full meaning, must have a higher motive than getting. Perhaps because they were reared in greater affluence than the two previous generations—the depression generation and the World War II generation—they seem to grasp more clearly the eternal truth that getting is important but by itself is not enough.

Christian missionaries of the last century made enormous personal sacrifice that changed the face of our world. Those missionaries dug the foundations for the explosive growth of Christian faith that is now happening in Africa, South America, Korea, and across the world. Ted Engstrom, one of the developers of World Vision—an organization that has done so much to feed millions of the world's starving—raised a good question for all of us in *Christian Leadership Letter.*

> In the nineteenth century era of missions, missionaries sailed for the unknown, well aware that nineteen out of twenty of them would die before returning home. They knew what they were heading into. They took their families with them, knowing that perhaps they would have to bury their children in a strange land. But they were convinced that they were going where God had called them to go, and obedience was more important than life itself. What ever happened to that kind of commitment?[4]

The answer to that question is found in the new consensus among young adults. People are rediscovering Jesus' insight. Life has far greater possibilities than merely being alive, loving our families, doing our work, and enjoying our leisure. Life has a spiritual dimension, which Jesus called the kingdom of God. When we enter it, we reach out in service to others and find that life overflows with meaning. When we do not enter it, we find that meaning drains away through the holes in our self-serving.

One-Tenth Is not Enough

Mention the word *stewardship,* and people think of money. The discussion usually turns to matters such as tithing, pledging to the church, and "how much is enough?" Years of using the word *stewardship* in a limited way naturally leads us toward defining religious selfishness as not contributing enough money to the church. We are right in the sense that withholding money is a frequent symptom of selfishness. But when Jesus speaks of self-giving, he is talking about much more than money. For Jesus, stewardship involves the way we spend ten-tenths of our life, not just one-tenth.

A pastor tells of standing by his father's tombstone and reading the words "Born 1884–Died 1970." It suddenly occurred to him how much the little dash between those two dates symbolized.

An entire life was wrapped up in one little straight line between two numbers.

Someday, a tombstone will rest above all our heads. A dash will represent whatever we stood for and did. It can have a great deal of meaning or not much, depending on what we decide to do with it. We are all born. We all die. There is not much we can do to change that. But we can build a great deal of meaning into the dash in between, and a major part of that meaning comes through the verb *serve*.

Discovery Questions for Group Study

1. Is the giving of our money to serve God's causes as important as the giving of our time and energy?
2. The "Catching Our Own Passes" section lists three positive results that come from serving. Can you think of others?
3. Do you agree or disagree with the idea that our serving should involve giving 10 percent of our income to God's work?
4. Among the questions listed in the "To Be Specific" section, do you think any stand out as having particular relevance for Christians in your local community? In your congregation? In your denomination?
5. Distribute Bibles and study the passages listed with each "serve" sample from Jesus' teachings. What point did these words make to people in Jesus' day? What do these words say to you personally? What do these words say to contemporary Christians and contemporary churches?

NOTES

1. Repent: Winning Is Not Enough!

1. *Pulpit Helps,* vol. 12, no. 9 (June 1987).
2. Albert Henry Newman, *A Manual of Church History,* vol. 1 (Philadelphia: Judson, 1899), p. 307.
3. "Expiation." *Philosophical Dictionary* (1764).
4. Charles L. Allen, *Joyful Living in the Fourth Dimension* (Old Tappan, N.J.: Fleming H. Revell Company, 1983), p. 76.

2. Follow: Leadership Is Not Enough!

1. Excerpts of a speech reported in the *Chicago Tribune* and printed in *The Presbyterian Layman.*
2. Quote from a brochure by E. Stanley Jones Associates for Evangelism. No copyright date available.
3. "Methodists Luring New Members." *Lubbock Avalanche Journal* (February 8, 1987)
4. Lloyd J. Ogilvie, *The Other Jesus* (Waco, Texas: Word, Incorporated), 1986.
5. William G. Chrystal, *The Fellowship of Prayer* (St. Louis: CBP Press), 1987.

3. Pray: Wired for Electricity?

1. Auguste Sabatier, *Outlines of a Philosophy of Religion Based on Psychology and History,* trans. T. A. Seed (New York: Harper Torchbooks, 1957), p. 25.
2. *U.S. News & World Report* (April 13, 1987): 42.
3. E. Stanley Jones, *A Song of Ascents* (Nashville: Abingdon Press, 1968), p. 72.
4. From a speech delivered at the eighth annual Church Growth International Conference in Seoul, Korea, July 7-13, 1987.

4. Believe: Prayer Is Almost Enough

1. John Wesley, "To Miss March." In *Through the Year with Wesley,* comp. and ed. Frederick C. Gill (Nashville: The Upper Room, 1983), p. 72.
2. *1980 Lent Devotional Booklet,* First Christian Church, Borger, Texas (mimeo).
3. T. H. Tappert, ed., *Luther Letters of Spiritual Counsel* (LCCI) (Philadelphia: Westminster Press, 1955), pp. 146-47.

4. "Financial Insecurity Dominates Americans' Family Worries." *Emerging Trends*, vol. 9, no. 9 (November 1987):3.

5. "Performance-Building Advice from the Consummate Pro." *Voices of Experience* audio cassette series. Interview with Bill Gove at the 1987 National Speakers Association Meeting, Phoenix, Arizona.

6. Leslie D. Weatherhead, *Psychology, Religion, and Healing* (New York: Abingdon Press, 1951), p. 431.

5. Love: God with Skin on

1. Archibald Macleish, *Time* (December 22, 1958).

2. J. Kenneth Kimberlin, "Preaching on the Lessons." *The Clergy Journal*, vol. LVII (September 1981):19-24.

3. "I Had a Dream. . . ." *PMA Advisor* (May 1987):2.

4. George Parsons, "A Language of Caring Spoken Here." *Action Information* (March/April 1987):1.

5. "Church on the Rock to Celebrate First Year." *Lubbock Avalanche-Journal* (December 12, 1987):12C.

6. See Dan McCrory, "Calling All South Africa to Repent." *Eternity* (April 1987):13.

7. See Charles Mylander, "Living on the Growing Edge." *Quaker Life* (May 1987):37.

8. David McKay in pastor's column of church newsletter, Brentwood Christian Church (Disciples of Christ), *The Brentwood Visitor*, Springfield, Missouri (June 30, 1987) (mimeo).

6. Forgive: The Ultimate Character Test

1. C. Thomas Hilton, "Do You Love Me?" *The Clergy Journal*, vol. LXI, no. 10 (September 1985):28.

2. W. E. Sangster, *Sangster's Special Day Sermons* (New York: Abingdon Press, 1960), p. 31.

3. Henry G. Bosch, "Clean In a Dirty Place." In *Our Daily Bread*, vol. 32, nos. 9, 10, 11 (Grand Rapids: Radio Bible Class, 1987).

4. Richard W. DeHaan, "No Grudges After Sunset." In *Our Daily Bread*, vol. 31, no. 12; vol. 32, nos. 1, 2 (Grand Rapids: Radio Bible Class, 1987).

7. Go: Salt Shaker Suggestions

1. *The Brentwood Visitor*, Brentwood Christian Church (Disciples of Christ), Springfield, Missouri (mimeo).

2. Al Broom and Lorraine Broom, *One-to-One Discipling*, Church Dynamics, International School of Theology, Arrowhead Springs, P.O. Box 50015, San Bernardino, California 92412.

8. Baptize: God's Wedding Ring

1. Roger Russ, "The 'One Baptism.' " *NZ Christian* (November 1987).

9. Teach: Lamplighter Power

1. Herbert Butterfield, *Christianity and History* (London: G. Bell & Sons, Ltd., 1950), p. 131.

2. Kate Greer, "Are American Families Finding New Strength in Spirituality?" *Better Homes and Gardens* (January 1988):21.

3. Paul Robbins, "From the Office of the Publisher." *Leadership*, vol. VI, no. 2 (Spring 1985).

4. November 15, 1982, newsletter, First Christian Church (Disciples of Christ, Liberal, Kansas) (mimeo).

10. Serve: God's Personnel

1. "Interview with Orion Hutchinson." *Newscope* (January 9, 1987):3.

2. "Demo Memo." *American Demographics* (August 1987):4.

3. "Steady Increase Noted in Percent of Volunteers in U.S." *Emerging Trends*, vol. 9, no. 6 (June 1987):2.

4. *Christian Leadership Letter*, published by World Vision, date unknown.